Mac OS® X Leopard™ Just the Steps™ FOR DUMMIES®

by Keith Underdahl

1807 WILEY 2007
BICENTENNIAL

Wiley Publishing, Inc.

Mac OS® X Leopard™ Just the Steps™ For Dummies®

Published by
Wiley Publishing, Inc.
111 River Street
Hoboken, NJ 07030-5774

www.wiley.com

Copyright © 2007 by Wiley Publishing, Inc., Indianapolis, Indiana

Published by Wiley Publishing, Inc., Indianapolis, Indiana

Published simultaneously in Canada

For general information on our other products and services, please contact our Customer Care Department within the U.S. at 800-762-2974, out-side the U.S. at 317-572-3993, or fax 317-572-4002.

For technical support, please visit www.wiley.com/techsupport.

Wiley also publishes its books in a variety of electronic formats. Some content that appears in print may not be available in electronic books.

Library of Congress Control Number: 2007920005

ISBN: 978-0-470-10967-0

Manufactured in the United States of America

10 9 8 7 6 5 4 3 2 1

WILEY

About the Author

Keith Underdahl is a graphic designer, electronic publishing specialist, and freelance writer from Oregon. He has written numerous books, including *Digital Video For Dummies 4th Edition, Adobe Premiere Elements For Dummies, Wi-Fi Home Networking Just the Steps For Dummies*, and more.

Author's Acknowledgments

First and foremost, I wish to thank my family for their patience as I introduced Macs into our home for the first time. I have been using Macintosh computers in my work for over a decade, but having them at home was new and there was some initial skepticism. Fortunately, it didn't take long for everyone to realize that these Macs actually do work pretty well!

I want to thank Bob Woerner and Wiley for bringing me on for this book, and the Wiley publishing team who helped put it all together. Nicole Sholly and Jennifer Riggs turned my cocktail napkin scribblings into something readable, and Dennis Cohen made sure that it was all technically accurate.

I also received assistance from Andy Marken and Bob "Dr. Mac" LeVitus. Thanks folks!

Publisher's Acknowledgments

We're proud of this book; please send us your comments through our online registration form located at www.dummies.com/register/. Some of the people who helped bring this book to market include the following:

Acquisitions, Editorial, and Media Development

Project Editor: Nicole Sholly

Senior Acquisitions Editor: Bob Woerner

Copy Editor: Jennifer Riggs

Technical Editor: Dennis R. Cohen

Editorial Manager: Kevin Kirschner

Editorial Assistant: Amanda Foxworth

Sr. Editorial Assistant: Cherie Case

Cartoons: Rich Tennant (www.the5thwave.com)

Composition Services

Project Coordinator: Kristie Rees

Layout and Graphics: Stacie Brooks, Melanee Prendergast, Brent Savage, Erin Zeltner

Proofreader: Sossity R. Smith

Indexer: Rebecca R. Plunkett

Anniversary Logo Design: Richard Pacifico

Publishing and Editorial for Technology Dummies

Richard Swadley, Vice President and Executive Group Publisher

Andy Cummings, Vice President and Publisher

Mary Bednarek, Executive Acquisitions Director

Mary C. Corder, Editorial Director

Publishing for Consumer Dummies

Diane Graves Steele, Vice President and Publisher

Joyce Pepple, Acquisitions Director

Composition Services

Gerry Fahey, Vice President of Production Services

Debbie Stailey, Director of Composition Services

Contents at a Glance

Mac users have always been a loyal group, and for good reasons. Since Apple first started producing Macintosh computers in the 1980s, they've placed an emphasis on quality, ease-of-use, and stability. Modern Macs running the latest OS X operating system are among the most powerful and dependable personal computers you can buy, and they're versatile enough to meet virtually any personal or professional need you may have.

About This Book

Macs are user friendly, but they're still computers, so you must follow certain steps to complete tasks, like setting up an e-mail account, accessing a Wi-Fi hotspot, transferring music to an iPod, customizing the OS X interface, creating a network, and almost any other computer task you can imagine. This book provides the steps you need to get running quickly, without having to pour through extra narratives or examples that you probably don't need anyway. And because a picture is worth a thousand words, all the steps in this book are accompanied by figures that walk you visually through each task.

Why You Need This Book

Whether you're new to Macs or you just want a handy quick reference to OS X Leopard, this book helps you get to work quickly and efficiently. Each task covers a specific subject, and most steps take only a minute or two to follow. This book also provides crucial tips that you won't find in your Mac's built-in help system.

Introduction

Conventions used in this book

➥ When you have to access a menu command, I use the ➪ symbol. For example, if you have to open the File menu and then choose Open, I say File➪Open.

➥ Internet addresses are presented like `www.dummies.com`. I leave off the `http://` part of Web addresses because you usually don't have to type it anyway.

 When you see this icon, the text includes helpful tips or extra information relating to the task.

How This Book Is Organized

I organized the chapters of this book into several basic parts:

Part I: Using OS X

The Mac OS X operating system is accessible and easy to use right out of the box. But if you want to customize the way OS X looks and behaves, the chapters in this part show you how. Chapters also show you how to manage system preferences and work with files and folders, which is especially helpful if you're new to Macs.

Part II: Getting to Work in OS X

Macs aren't all about iPods and movies. This part shows you how to use some of the handy programs that are included with OS X, as well as how to use productivity programs, such as word processors and presentation programs. I show you how to use and customize the OS X *Dashboard*, an innovative tool that gives you instant access to notepads, calculators, weather updates, sports scores, and more. And I show you how to clean up desktop clutter with Spaces, a new feature in OS X Leopard.

Part III: Going Online with Your Mac

If you're like most people, the Internet is one of the main reasons you use a computer in the first place. In this part, I show you how to browse the Web, exchange e-mail, chat, and even create your own blogs and Web pages.

Part IV: Using Multimedia

A modern Mac running OS X Leopard is one of the most powerful multimedia devices you can buy. With iLife programs that come free with most new Macs, you can watch DVDs, manage and play your music library, send music to iPods and other MP3 players, organize and improve digital photos, and make your own movies.

Part V: Networking Your Mac

If you have more than one computer, you'll probably want to connect those computers together at some point so that they can share files, printers, Internet connections, and other resources. This part shows you how to set up networks between all your computers, even if some of those computers are Windows PCs.

Part VI: Extending Your Mac's Capabilities

As powerful and versatile as most Macs are, they can be even more. In this part, I show you how to use Bluetooth peripherals with your Mac, how to network with computers running older versions of the Macintosh operating system, and how to upgrade your Mac. One chapter even shows you how to install the Microsoft Windows operating system on your Mac, a new capability with Intel-chipped Macs running OS X Leopard.

Get Ready To

If you're ready to fire up your first Mac, or you're a long-time user and need quick steps to access advanced features, there's a task in this book that's ready to help you.

Part 1
Using OS X

Customizing OS X

Apple is rightfully proud of the user interface design incorporated into the Macintosh OS X family of operating systems. The interface is easy to use, and it's also easy to customize so that your Mac looks and behaves the way you want.

This chapter shows you how to customize various parts of the OS X interface, including

→ **Desktop:** You can change the color scheme of your desktop or use a picture as your background.

→ **Display:** You can also change the size of the desktop display, use a custom screen saver, and adjust the way the clock appears.

→ **Dock:** The OS X Dock normally resides at the bottom of the screen and gives quick access to your most commonly used programs. You can move the Dock, add or remove items, and change the way the Dock appears.

→ **Keyboard and Accessibility:** Mac OS X can accommodate most accessibility needs, and common keyboard shortcuts can be changed, too.

→ **Exposé:** Switch quickly between programs with this OS X tool.

→ **Spaces:** If you're tired of constantly re-arranging your desktop, create and easily move between multiple virtual workspaces using Leopard's new Spaces feature.

Chapter

1

Get ready to . . .

Access System Preferences

1. Open the Apple menu by clicking the Apple icon in the upper-left corner of the screen.

2. Choose System Preferences from the Apple menu to reveal the System Preferences screen, as shown in Figure 1-1.

    You can also open System Preferences from the Dock.

3. Click a preference icon to open a group of settings.

    To return to the main System Preferences window, click the Show All button at the top of any individual settings screen.

Modify the Desktop Appearance

1. Open System Preferences and then click the Appearance icon.

2. Click the Appearance menu and then choose a color scheme for the overall appearance of the interface (see Figure 1-2).

3. Click the Highlight Color menu and choose a highlight color for selected text.

4. Use the Place Scroll Arrows radio buttons to choose whether you want scroll arrows right next to each other or placed at the top and bottom of scroll bars.

5. Select other scroll bar options as desired.

    If you find that your computer freezes momentarily or responds slowly when scrolling through documents, deselect the Use Smooth Scrolling option.

Figure 1-1: Start with the System Preferences window to change OS X settings.

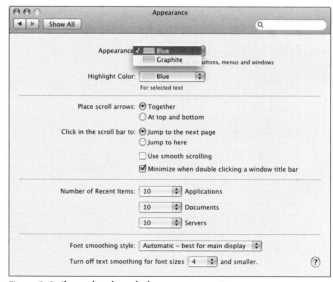

Figure 1-2: Change the color and other appearance settings.

6. Choose the maximum number of items that are displayed in Recent Items menus for Applications, Documents, and Servers.

7. Click Show All to return to the main System Preferences screen.

8. Click the Desktop & Screen Saver icon.

9. In the Desktop & Screen Saver settings window that appears, click the Desktop button to bring Desktop settings to the front (see Figure 1-3), if they aren't shown already.

10. Click an image folder on the left side of the settings window and then choose a picture or swatch on the right to use as your desktop background. Choices include

   - **Apple Images:** These are standard background graphics supplied with OS X.

   - **Themed images:** OS X also includes stock photos of nature scenes, plants, and other things, which can be used as desktop backgrounds.

   - **Solid Colors:** Choose a color swatch to make your desktop background a solid color.

   - **Pictures Folder:** Click this to use any image from your Pictures folder, as shown in Figure 1-4.

11. Using the menu at the top of the Desktop window, choose whether you want to tile smaller images or stretch them to fill the whole screen.

 Enable the Change Picture check box at the bottom of the screen to automatically change the background image periodically. By using this feature, you can turn your desktop into a slide show.

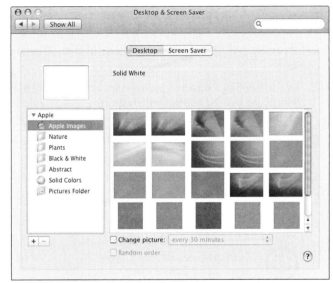

Figure 1-3: Click the Desktop button to bring desktop settings to the front.

Figure 1-4: You can use almost any picture as your desktop background.

Change the Display Size

1. Open System Preferences and then click the Displays icon.

2. In the Displays screen that appears, click the Display button to bring Display settings to the front, if they aren't shown already.

3. Choose a resolution on the left side of the screen, as shown in Figure 1-5.

4. Use the Brightness slider to adjust the display brightness.

5. Choose a Colors setting and a Refresh Rate in each respective menu.

 In general, you should use the highest available settings in the Colors and Refresh Rate menus. Reduce them only if you see distortion or other display problems.

 If you connect a second display to your computer — for example, an external monitor or a multimedia projector — open the Displays settings and then click the Detect Displays button. OS X detects the new display and allows you to adjust its settings as well.

6. Click the Color button to bring the Color settings to the front, as shown in Figure 1-6.

7. Choose a Display Profile on the left side of the screen.

 Which Display Profile you use depends primarily on your hardware. See Chapter 4 for more on choosing display profiles.

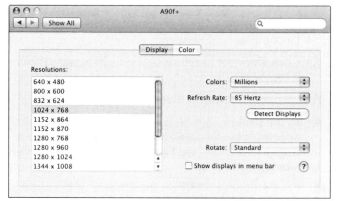

Figure 1-5: Change the display resolution and brightness here.

Figure 1-6: Choose a color profile for your display.

Customize Keyboard Shortcuts

1. Quit any open applications by using ⌘+Q.

2. Open System Preferences and then click the Keyboard & Mouse icon to open the Keyboard & Mouse settings, as shown in Figure 1-7.

3. Click the Keyboard Shortcuts button to bring Keyboard Shortcut settings to the front, as shown in Figure 1-8.

4. Scroll down the list of available commands to find the one you want to customize.

5. Double-click the shortcut you want to change. Make sure you double-click the actual shortcut listed in the Shortcut column, not the command listed in the Description column.

6. Press the new keyboard shortcut that you want to use for the command.

 If the shortcut you want to use is assigned already to a different command, a yellow warning triangle appears next to the duplicated shortcuts. If you see the yellow warning triangles, at least one shortcut must be changed.

7. To disable a keyboard shortcut, remove the check mark next to it in the On column.

8. Close the Keyboard & Mouse preferences window to save your changes.

 If you're unhappy with the keyboard shortcuts you've customized or if you're using a pre-owned computer that was customized by someone else, open the Keyboard Shortcuts settings and click the Restore Defaults button. This restores all keyboard shortcuts back to their factory defaults.

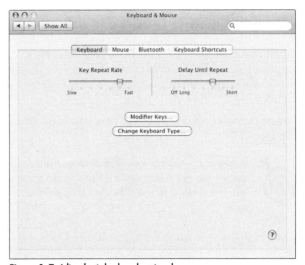

Figure 1-7: Adjust basic keyboard settings here.

Figure 1-8: Keyboard shortcuts are customized easily.

Add and Remove Dock Items

1. Open the icon for your hard drive and then click Applications in the sidebar on the left side of the Finder window to open the Applications folder, as shown in Figure 1-9.

2. Locate the icon for the program that you want to add to the Dock.

    In some cases — such as Apple iWork or Microsoft Office applications — you may need to open a subfolder to find a program's icon. Look closely at the icon; if the icon looks like a folder, it is a folder.

3. Click and drag the program's icon to the Dock, as shown in Figure 1-9. The place where you drop the icon on the Dock will be that icon's location, so choose a location carefully.

4. To launch an application from the Dock, simply click the appropriate icon. The application launches.

5. To remove an item from the Dock, click-and-hold the mouse pointer on the item until a pop-up menu appears, as shown in Figure 1-10.

    If you're using a two-button mouse, simply right-click the Dock icon you want to remove instead of clicking-and-holding.

6. While still holding down the mouse button, move the pointer over Remove from Dock and then release the mouse button. The item disappears from the Dock.

Figure 1-9: Click and drag application icons to the Dock.

Figure 1-10: Items can be removed from the Dock as easily as they are added.

Move and Hide the Dock

1. Open System Preferences and then click the Dock icon.

2. In the Dock settings screen, as shown in Figure 1-11, move the Dock Size slider to change the Dock size.

   You can also change the Dock size at any time by clicking and dragging up or down on the thin vertical line near the right side of the Dock.

3. If you want to use Dock magnification — useful if you have the Dock size set to small and it holds many icons — place a check mark next to Magnification and adjust the slider as desired.

4. Choose a Dock position by clicking the Left, Bottom, or Right radio buttons. Figure 1-12 shows the Dock on the left side of the screen.

   If you have a widescreen monitor, you may find that putting the Dock on the left or right side of the screen makes more efficient use of screen real estate.

5. If you don't like the bouncy feedback provided by Dock icons when you launch a program, remove the check mark next to Animate Opening Applications. An arrow still shows you when the program is launching.

6. To automatically hide the Dock when it isn't in use, place a check mark next to Automatically Hide and Show the Dock. To reveal the hidden Dock, simply move the mouse pointer to the bottom (or left or right, as appropriate) of the screen.

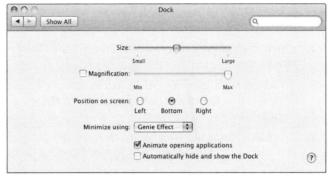

Figure 1-11: You can customize many aspects of the Dock.

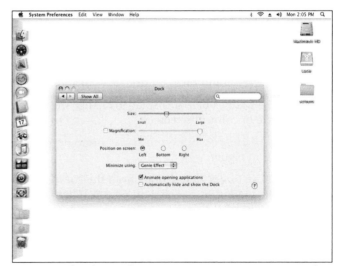

Figure 1-12: If you have a widescreen monitor, you may want to move your Dock to the side.

Make OS X Accessible

1. Open System Preferences and then click the Universal Access icon.

2. To adjust settings for visual impairments, click the Seeing tab to reveal the Seeing settings, as shown in Figure 1-13.

3. To enable *VoiceOver* — a basic screen reader program built-in to OS X — select the On radio button below VoiceOver.

 If you aren't happy with how VoiceOver sounds, click the Open VoiceOver Utility button. There you can change the voice, pitch, speed, and other characteristics of VoiceOver.

4. To enable screen zooming, select the On radio button below Zoom. Press Option+⌘+= to zoom in on an area of the screen, and press Option+⌘+- to zoom back out.

5. Use the settings below Display to change the appearance and use of color onscreen.

6. Click the Hearing button to reveal audio options, as shown in Figure 1-14.

7. If you can't hear alert sounds from the computer, place a check mark next to Flash the Screen When an Alert Sound Occurs.

 Click the Flash Screen button to test the screen flash.

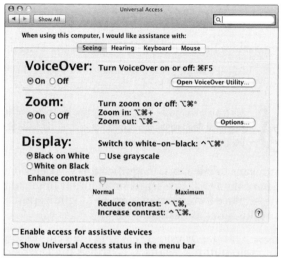

Figure 1-13: Use these settings if you need help seeing your Mac.

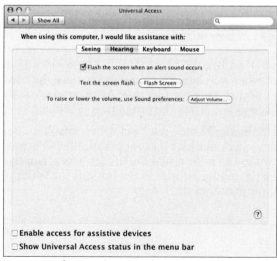

Figure 1-14: If you can't hear audio alerts, you can enable a screen flash instead.

8. Click the Keyboard button to adjust keyboard options, as shown in Figure 1-15.

9. To enable Sticky Keys, select the On radio button next to Sticky Keys. Sticky Keys allows you to use modifier keys, such as Shift, Function, Control, Option, and ⌘, without simultaneously pressing multiple keys.

> If you need Sticky Keys only occasionally, place a check mark next to Press the Shift Key Five Times to Turn Sticky Keys On or Off. This option gives you an easy way to quickly enable or disable Sticky Keys.

10. To create a delay between when a key is first pressed and when it's accepted by the computer, click On next to Slow Keys. Use the Acceptance Delay slider to change the length of the delay.

11. Click Mouse & Trackpad to open pointer device settings, as shown in Figure 1-16.

12. If you wish to use a numeric keypad in place of a mouse, click On next to Mouse Keys.

> If your keyboard doesn't include a dedicated keypad — this is usually the case with laptops — you can purchase a USB (Universal Series Bus) keypad at most computer and office supply stores.

13. Use the Initial Delay and Maximum Speed sliders to fine-tune the behavior of Mouse Keys.

14. If the mouse cursor is too small, use the Cursor Size slider to change the size of the cursor. The Cursor Size slider works with Mouse Keys as well as a conventional mouse or trackpad.

> If you're giving a presentation with your Mac and a digital projector, you may want to increase the size of the mouse cursor so that the cursor can be used as an onscreen pointer during the presentation.

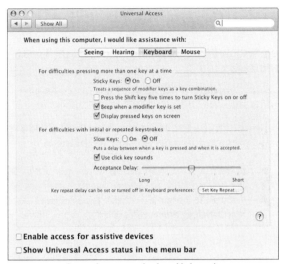

Figure 1-15: Change the way your keyboard behaves here.

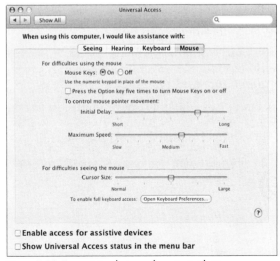

Figure 1-16: Your pointing device can be customized, too.

Activate a Screen Saver

1. Open System Preferences and then click the Desktop & Screen Saver icon.

2. Click the Screen Saver button to reveal screen saver settings, as shown in Figure 1-17.

3. Scroll through the list of screen savers and click a screen saver to preview it in the window to the right.

     To create a screen saver with photos from your iPhoto library, choose Library in the Screen Savers list. Alternatively, scroll down the Screen Savers list and click Choose Folder and then browse to a folder containing pictures you want to use.

4. Use the Start Screen Saver slider to change when the screen saver appears. If you choose 15, for example, the screen saver appears only after the computer is inactive for 15 minutes.

5. To configure a hot corner for activating your screen saver, click the Hot Corners button.

6. Decide which corner you want as the hot corner and then choose Start Screen Saver in that corner's menu, as shown in Figure 1-18.

7. Click OK to close the hot corner options. To test the hot corner, move the mouse pointer all the way to the corner you selected. The screen saver begins.

     If you don't want to use a screen saver, move the Start Screen Saver slider to Never.

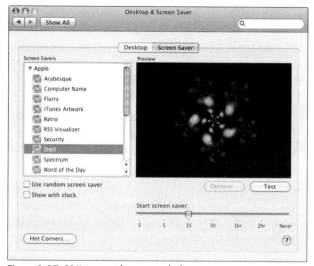

Figure 1-17: OS X comes with some neat built-in screen savers.

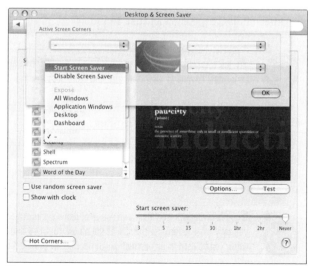

Figure 1-18: Hot corners can be used to quickly activate a screen saver.

Display 24-Hour Time

1. Open System Preferences and then click the Date & Time icon.

    You can also open the Date & Time control panel by clicking-and-holding the clock in the upper-right corner of the screen and then choosing Open Date & Time from the contextual menu that appears.

2. Click the Clock button to bring Clock preferences to the front, as shown in Figure 1-19.

3. Select Use a 24-Hour Clock to display time in 24-hour format.

    If you're displaying time in 24-hour format, it makes sense to deselect the Show AM/PM option.

4. Adjust other clock options as desired and then click the Date & Time button to show the calendar and time setting options, as shown in Figure 1-20.

    Some clock options — such as Analog display — aren't compatible with a 24-hour clock.

5. If you want the computer to automatically synchronize its clock with an online date and time source, make sure that Set Date & Time Automatically is checked. Choose a source based on your geographical location.

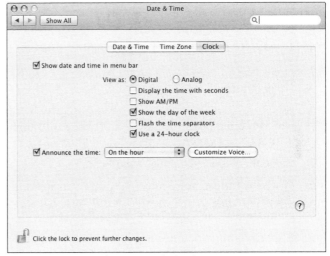

Figure 1-19: Customize the way time is displayed on your computer.

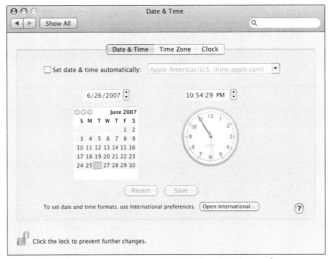

Figure 1-20: Your computer can automatically check and set the time for you.

Access Programs Quickly with Exposé

1. Open System Preferences and then click the Exposé & Spaces button.

2. Select a hot corner that you want to use for switching between open programs and then choose All Windows in that corner's menu, as shown in Figure 1-21.

3. Close the Exposé & Spaces window.

4. Move the mouse pointer to the corner you selected as the Exposé hot corner. A window for each active program appears, as shown in Figure 1-22.

5. Click the program window you want to open. The selected program becomes active although those other programs are still running.

You can also quickly switch between open applications by holding down the ⌘ key and then pressing Tab. A small window appears in the middle of the screen with an icon for each open application. Keep pressing Tab until the desired program is highlighted and then release the ⌘ key.

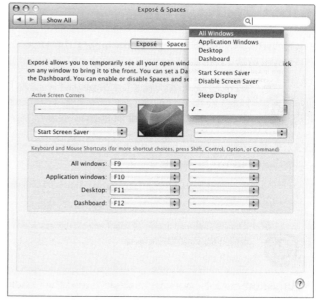

Figure 1-21: Select a hot corner here.

Figure 1-22: Click the program window you want to open.

Set up Spaces

1. Open System Preferences and then click the Exposé & Spaces icon.

2. Click the Spaces button to open Spaces options, as shown in Figure 1-23.

3. Place a check mark next to Enable Spaces.

 To switch between Spaces more easily, place a check mark next to Show Spaces in Menu Bar. A Spaces number appears in the menu bar. Click the Space number and then select a new space from the menu that appears to jump to that space.

4. To add spaces, click the plus sign next to either Column or Row. In Figure 1-23, one row has been added.

5. If you want to use only a certain program in a certain space — for example, you may set up a separate space just for the DVD player — click the plus sign under Application Bindings.

6. In the Finder window that appears, as shown in Figure 1-24, select an application and then click Add.

7. In the Application Bindings column of the Spaces window, click the Space number and choose a space to which the application should be assigned.

 You can create bindings for any application, but they're most effective for multimedia applications that might compete with each other, such as iTunes and the DVD Player. If iTunes is in Space 3, audio from iTunes goes away when you switch to the DVD Player in Space 4 and vice versa.

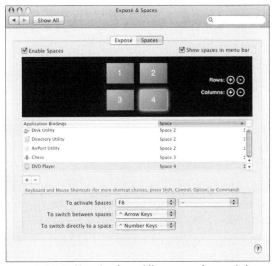

Figure 1-23: Enable and configure different spaces for your desktop.

Figure 1-24: Applications can be assigned to specific spaces.

Switch between Spaces

1. To switch between spaces, use one of the following techniques:

   - Press F8 to activate spaces, as shown in Figure 1-25, and then click the space that you want to open.

    You can change the Spaces hot key by opening the Spaces preferences window and selecting a different function key from the To Activate Spaces menu. F8 is the default hot key for spaces.

   - Click the Spaces number in the menu bar (if shown) and then select a Space number from the menu that appears.

   - Launch a program that has a dependency to a specific space. The previous section shows you how to set up dependencies.

2. To move an application window from one space to another, activate Spaces and then click and drag a window to a new space, as shown in Figure 1-26.

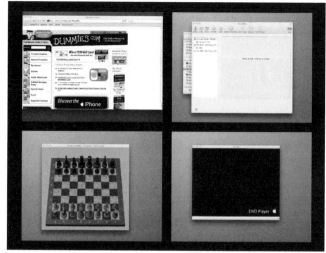

Figure 1-25: Press F8 to activate spaces and then click a space to open it.

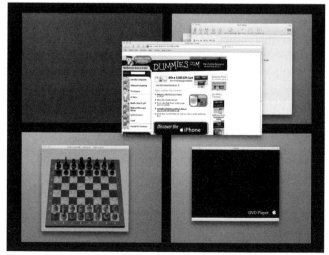

Figure 1-26: You can click and drag application windows between Spaces.

Creating and Managing User Accounts

After you get a new computer, one of the first things you will probably do is customize it to fit your needs and personality. You may customize the desktop appearance, add your favorite programs to the Dock, and set up e-mail and chat programs for your personal accounts. But what if your new computer is shared by other people? They may want to do customizations of their own, and you probably don't want other people using your e-mail account.

The Macintosh operating system allows you to easily set up multiple user accounts on your computer. Personal user accounts have several advantages:

⟶ Each user can customize the way the operating system looks and behaves without affecting other users.

⟶ Users can set up and use their own e-mail and Internet accounts.

⟶ Private files and communications stay private.

⟶ User accounts can help prevent unauthorized persons from using the computer.

⟶ Parents can control how their children spend their time on the computer.

This chapter shows you how to set up and manage user accounts on your computer.

Disable Automatic Login

1. Open System Preferences and then click the Accounts icon.

2. Click Login Options.

3. Click the Lock icon in the lower-left corner and then enter your administrator password to unlock changes.

4. In the Automatic Login menu choose Disabled, as shown in Figure 2-1.

5. Under Display Login Window As, choose one of the following options:

   • **List of users:** A list of users appears in the login window. Users click a name and then enter a password to login.

   • **Name and password:** The login window simply shows empty Name and Password fields. This option is less convenient but slightly more secure.

Require a Password to Wake the Computer

1. Open System Preferences and then click the Security icon.

2. Click the System button.

3. Place a check mark next to Require Password to Wake This Computer from Sleep or Screen Saver; see Figure 2-2.

 If you haven't already disabled Automatic Login, a warning message suggests that you do so if you require a password to wake the computer from sleep or a screen saver.

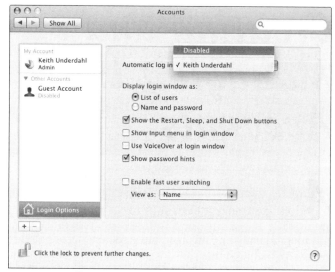

Figure 2-1: Disable Automatic Login to make your computer more secure.

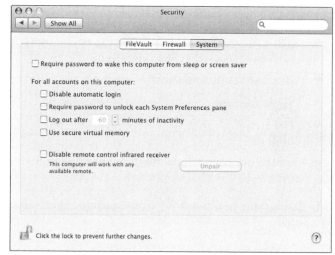

Figure 2-2: Use the Security control panel to require passwords at login.

Create a New User Account

1. Open System Preferences and then click the Accounts icon.

2. Click the Lock icon in the lower-left corner of the Accounts control panel and then enter your administrator password to unlock account settings.

3. Click the plus sign in the lower-left corner — just above the Lock icon — of the Accounts window. The new account tab appears, as shown in Figure 2-3.

4. Enter a name and a short name for the account.

   The short name is used for system folders. If you don't like the short name that's generated automatically, change it now because the short name can't be changed after the account is created.

5. Enter a password and a password hint for the new user.

   If you're not sure whether your password is secure enough, click the key button next to the Password field to open the Password Assistant. The Assistant grades the quality of your password and suggests alternatives if necessary.

6. Choose an account type in the Account Type menu.

   Administrator rights allow you to create new accounts, install programs, and change other important system settings, so choose carefully when deciding who will and will not get administrator rights on your computer. Most accounts should be Standard or Managed with Parental Controls. Sharing accounts give read-only access and should mainly be used for remote network users.

7. Click Create Account. The new account appears in the accounts list, as shown in Figure 2-4.

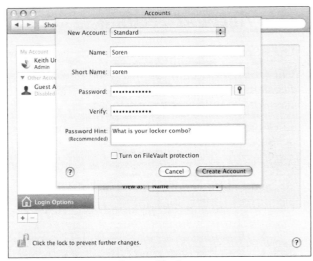

Figure 2-3: Enter a name and password for the new account.

Figure 2-4: New accounts appear in the list on the left.

Change Account Settings

1. Open System Preferences and then click the Accounts icon.

2. Click the Lock icon in the lower-left corner of the Accounts control panel and enter your administrator password to unlock account settings.

3. Click the account name for which you want to change settings.

4. Adjust basic account settings, such as administrator rights.

5. To change the account's picture, click the Picture.

6. Choose a picture in the list, as shown in Figure 2-5.

 If you want to use your own picture, click Edit Picture and then click Choose in the Images window that appears. Browse to the photo you want to use. If your computer has an iSight or built-in camera, you'll also be given the option to take a picture using it.

Change a Password

1. Open System Preferences and then click the Accounts icon.

2. Click the Lock icon in the lower-left corner of the Accounts control panel and enter your administrator password to unlock account settings.

3. Click the account name for which you want to change the password and then click Reset Password.

4. In the Reset Password window that appears, as shown in Figure 2-6, enter a new password and a hint.

5. Click Reset Password to set the new password.

Figure 2-5: Choose an account picture here.

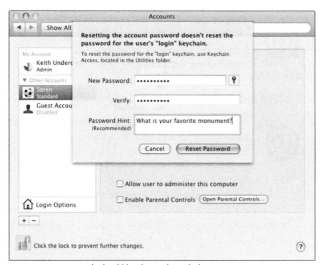

Figure 2-6: Passwords should be changed regularly.

Switch between User Accounts

1. Open System Preferences and then click the Accounts icon.

2. Click the Lock icon in the lower-left corner of the Accounts control panel and enter your administrator password to unlock account settings.

3. Click Login Options at the bottom of the accounts list.

4. In the login options that appear, place a check mark next to Enable Fast User Switching, as shown in Figure 2-7.

5. Choose how you want users to appear on the switching menu — Name, Short Name, or Icon Image — and then close the Accounts window.

 Fast user switching makes it easier to switch between users, but it isn't necessary. Don't enable fast user switching if your computer has limited memory or you don't want to allow multiple users to log in simultaneously.

6. To switch to a different user, click the user name in the upper-right corner of the menu bar.

7. In the User Switching menu that appears, as shown in Figure 2-8, choose a user name to switch to that user.

 If you don't enable fast user switching, you must log out of the current account before switching to a new user. Choose Apple⇨Log Out to log out of the current account and then use the standard OS X login screen to log in to a different account.

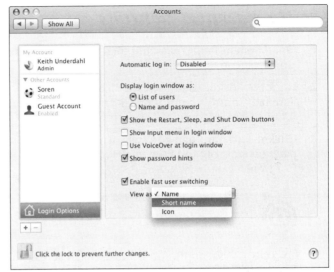

Figure 2-7: Enable fast user switching in the Login Options window.

Figure 2-8: Click the user name to switch to a new user.

Set Up Parental Controls

1. Open System Preferences and then click the Parental Controls icon.

2. Click the Lock icon in the lower-left corner of the Parental Controls control panel and enter your administrator password to unlock the settings.

3. Click the account name for which you want to set up parental controls and then click Enable Parental Controls.

 You can't set up parental controls on administrator accounts.

4. To control what applications the user can access, click System and then check or uncheck applications, as shown in Figure 2-9.

5. Place check marks next to system features that the user is allowed to use. In Figure 2-9, the user isn't allowed to burn CDs and DVDs or modify the Dock.

6. To limit who the person can correspond with by e-mail or iChat, click Mail & iChat and then place a check mark next to the services you want to limit.

7. In the e-mail address list, click the Add button (it looks like a plus sign) and then type the name and e-mail address that you want to allow.

8. Click Add to add the user to the list of allowable iChat or Mail partners, as shown in Figure 2-10.

Figure 2-9: Select which applications your child can use.

Figure 2-10: Use this window to control with whom your child exchanges e-mail.

9. To limit your child's access to adult Web sites or offensive content, click Content.

10. Place a check mark next to Hide Profanity in the Dictionary to block access to offensive words in the OS X Dictionary program.

11. Choose an option for limiting Web sites:

    • **Allow Unrestricted Access to Websites:** This option places no limits on Web site access.

    • **Try to Limit Access to Adult Website Automatically:** Safari attempts to identify and limit access to adult Web sites. This works most but not all the time.

    • **Allow Access to Only These Websites:** This reveals a list of Web sites, as shown in Figure 2-11. The user can visit only sites in this list. Click the plus sign under the list to add more Web sites.

12. To manage the amount of time your child spends on the computer, click Time Limits.

13. Place check marks next to Limit Computer Use To under Weekdays and Weekends and then use the sliders to set the maximum time, as shown in Figure 2-12.

14. Under Bedtime, place check marks next to School Nights and Weekends and then use the clock menus to set a bedtime for computer use.

Figure 2-11: Limit access to offensive Web sites and other material.

Figure 2-12: Control when and for how long your child uses the computer.

Delete a User Account

1. Back up any important files and data that may be stored in the user's personal folders.

   To back up the user's files, you will either need to log in to the computer as that user or use your administrator password to access the account.

2. Open System Preferences and then click the Accounts icon.

3. Click the Lock icon in the lower-left corner of the Accounts control panel and enter your administrator password to unlock account settings.

4. Click the user account name that you want to remove.

5. Click the Delete User button, which is located under the accounts list and looks like a minus sign.

6. Confirm that you actually want to delete the account, as shown in Figure 2-13.

   If you click OK, the user's files are retained. If you click Delete Immediately, all the user's files and settings are deleted immediately.

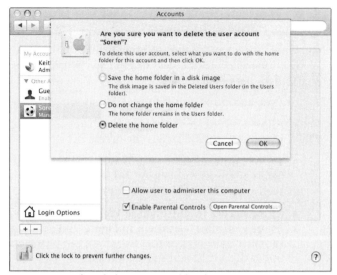

Figure 2-13: Confirm whether you want to delete the account.

Managing Files and Folders

Consider all the things for which you use your computer. You compose e-mail, browse the Internet, edit photos, play music, type memos, and more. Many of these tasks involve files that are stored on your hard drive.

The Macintosh operating system makes managing your files easy. The Mac OS X component that helps you browse and manage files is the *Finder*. The Finder runs at all times in the background, and you can open Finder windows from the Dock or any time you double-click the icon for a hard drive or folder. The Finder lets you quickly perform basic tasks, like creating folders and moving or deleting files. The Finder also lets you perform more advanced tasks, such as customizing a file's icon or changing the default program you use to open a file.

This chapter shows you how to manage files with the Finder. It also shows you how to use other OS X file management tools, including

- **Spotlight:** This is a powerful tool for searching files, programs, and even system settings.

- **Trash:** Deleted files are sent to the Trash. If you accidentally delete a needed file, you can usually recover it from the Trash.

- **Burn Folders:** Back up important files to recordable CDs or DVDs by using Burn folders.

- **Time Machine:** New in Leopard, Time Machine makes it easy to back up your entire computer on a regular basis.

Search Your Computer with Spotlight

1. Click the Spotlight icon in the upper-right corner of the OS X menu bar. The Spotlight icon looks like a magnifying glass.

2. Type a query. When you type, top results appear in a menu below Spotlight. Choose a result in the menu to open it.

3. To view a more detailed list of results, click Show All in the Spotlight menu to open the Spotlight window, as shown in Figure 3-1.

     To search a specific location (such as an external hard drive or your Pictures folder), select the location in the sidebar on the left side of the Spotlight window.

4. If Spotlight searches resources that you prefer not to search, open System Preferences and click the Spotlight icon.

     You can also open Spotlight Preferences by choosing Spotlight Preferences in the Spotlight menu.

5. In the Spotlight Preferences window, remove check marks next to resources that you don't want searched.

6. To block certain folders from being searched, click the Privacy button near the top of the Spotlight window.

7. Click Add (it looks like a plus sign) near the bottom of the Privacy window and then browse to the folder you want to block from being searched.

8. Select the folder and click Choose. The blocked folder appears in the list, as shown in Figure 3-2.

Figure 3-1: Use Spotlight to quickly search for files and other items.

Figure 3-2: You can block Spotlight from searching certain folders.

Associate Files with Different Programs

1. Open Finder and browse to a file for which you want to change the program association.

2. Click the file once to select it but don't double-click the file or open it.

3. With the file selected, press ⌘+I.

    You can also open the Info window by selecting the file and then choosing File⇨Get Info, or right-clicking the file and choosing Get Info from the menu that appears.

4. In the Info window, as shown in Figure 3-3, click the arrow next to Open With to expand the file opening options.

5. Click the menu under Open With and choose a different program.

    If you don't see the desired program listed in the menu, choose Other from the bottom of the menu and then browse the Applications folder to find the program you want to use to open the file.

    Make sure you select a program that is appropriate for opening the file. For example, if the file is a picture, you probably want to associate it with a graphics program like iPhoto or Adobe Photoshop. A word processing program, like Apple Pages, isn't the best program to open and edit photos in.

6. If you want to change the program association for all files of a given type, click Change All below the Open With menu.

7. Click Continue in the dialog box shown in Figure 3-4 to apply the global change.

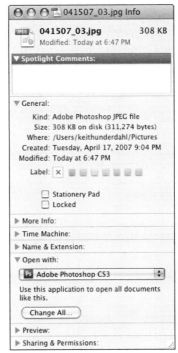

Figure 3-3: Use the Open With menu to change a file's program association.

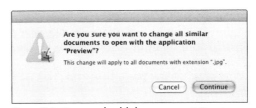

Figure 3-4: You can make global program associations, too.

Change a File's Icon

1. Open an image file containing the image you want to use as a file's icon.

    Ideally, the icon image should have some relevance to the document. For example, if the document is a PDF file containing information about your company, you may want to change the file's icon so that it uses your company logo.

2. Select the image and then copy it. If you're viewing the image in the OS X Preview program, simply choose Edit⇨Copy, as shown in Figure 3-5.

3. Close the image.

4. Open Finder and browse to a file for which you want to change the program association.

5. Click the file once to select it but don't double-click the file or open it.

6. With the file selected, press ⌘+I.

7. Click once on the current icon image in the upper-left corner of the Info window to select it.

8. With the old icon selected (a border appears around the icon when it is selected), as shown in Figure 3-6, press ⌘+V to paste in the new icon image.

9. Close the Info window. As you can see in Figure 3-6, the new icon image appears immediately in the Finder.

    You can follow these same steps to change a folder's icon as well as a file's icon.

Figure 3-5: Copy the image that you want to use as your new file icon.

Figure 3-6: To change a file's icon, simply paste in a new image.

Customize the Finder

1. Click the Finder button on the Dock to open a Finder window.

2. Click the options button (it looks like a toothed gear) and choose Show View Options.

    Make sure that no folder or file in the Finder is selected. If an item is selected, the Options menu lists commands specific to that item, and the Show View Options choice isn't available.

3. In the view options window that appears, customize appearance settings, such as icon sizes and labeling.

4. Close the view options window, and with the focus still on the Finder, choose Finder⟶Preferences.

5. Click Sidebar at the top of the Preferences window that appears and then remove check marks next to items that you don't want to appear in the Finder Sidebar, as shown in Figure 3-7. For example, if you don't use Apple's .Mac service, you may want to remove the check next to iDisk so it doesn't needlessly take up Finder space.

6. Close the Sidebar preferences and then with the focus still on the Finder, choose View⟶Customize Toolbar.

7. In the Toolbar Customization window that appears, as shown in Figure 3-8, click and drag buttons to the Finder toolbar. In Figure 3-8, I added the Separator, New Folder, Path, and Get Info buttons to the toolbar. Click Done after you're finished making changes.

    To remove items from the toolbar, simply click and drag them from the toolbar to the Tool Customization window. You can easily add them back later if you want.

Figure 3-7: Customize Finder sidebar items here.

Figure 3-8: You can easily add and remove Finder toolbar items.

Create Folders

1. Open the folder in which you want to create a sub-folder. If you want to create a new folder on the Desktop, click in an empty area of the Desktop to ensure it has the current focus.

2. Press ⌘+Shift+N to create a new folder. As you can see in Figure 3-9, the new folder is named Untitled Folder.

3. Type a new descriptive name for your folder.

 To keep your files secure, you should create subfolders only on the Desktop or in your user-specific folders in the Finder. User-specific folders in the Finder include Documents, Movies, Music, and Pictures. Each folder is represented by a link in the Finder Sidebar, so they're easy to find.

Rename Groups of Files

1. Make sure all the files you want to rename are together in a single folder. The folder should contain only the files you want to rename.

2. Open the Finder and then open the Applications folder.

3. In the Applications folder, open the AppleScript folder, open the Example Scripts folder, and then open the Finder Scripts folder. A list of Finder scripts appears, as shown in Figure 3-10.

4. To trim text from file names, double-click `Trim File Names.scpt`. The Script Editor launches.

Figure 3-9: Use folders and subfolders to organize your files.

 OS X comes with many handy scripts to help you automate various tasks. Poke around the AppleScript folder to find others that may be useful to you, but read the instructions for each script carefully to make sure you don't cause some damage.

Figure 3-10: Several Finder scripts help you rename groups of files.

5. Open the folder containing the files you want to modify.

Make sure that the folder containing the files you want to rename is in front of all other windows. The front-most window is the one to which the script is applied. If no folder window is open, the script renames files on the Desktop.

6. Click the Run button in the Script Editor window.

7. Enter the text string you want to trim from the file names, as shown in Figure 3-11.

8. If the text string is to be removed from the beginning of each file name, click Trim Start. Click Trim End if you want to trim the end of each file name.

9. To add text to the file names, open the `Add to File Names.scpt` script.

10. Confirm that the folder containing the files you want to rename is in front of all other windows.

11. Click Run in the Script Editor window.

12. Type the text string you want to add to the file names, as shown in Figure 3-12.

13. To add the string to the beginning of each file name, click Prefix. To add the string to the end, click Suffix.

14. After you're done running scripts and renaming files, click the Script Editor window and then press ⌘+Q to quit the Script Editor and ensure that scripts are not inadvertently run later.

If you're renaming files for use on a Web site, use the underscore character instead of spaces in the names. Also, remember that file names on the Internet are usually case sensitive.

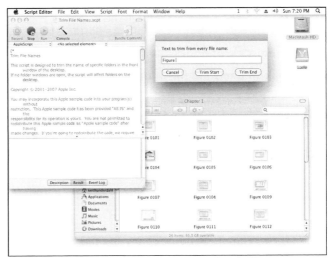

Figure 3-11: Enter the text string you want to remove from the file names.

Figure 3-12: Use the Add to File Names script to add text to file names.

Trash Files or Folders

1. Locate a file or folder that you want to delete.

2. Click and drag the file to the Trash icon on the Dock.

 If you have a two-button mouse, you can also right-click a file and choose Move to Trash from the contextual menu that appears.

 You can immediately undo an accidental trashing by pressing ⌘+Z or choosing Edit⇨Undo.

3. To see what's in the Trash, click the Trash icon on the Dock. A Finder window displaying the contents of the Trash appears, as shown in Figure 3-13.

4. If you want to restore an item from the Trash, click and drag the item to a new, safe location.

5. To empty the Trash, press ⌘+Shift+Delete or choose Finder⇨Empty Trash. You can empty the Trash only when the focus is on the Finder. If the focus is on another application, the ⌘+Shift+Delete command won't work.

6. When you see the confirmation warning, as shown in Figure 3-14, click OK. Items in the Trash are deleted permanently.

 If you're tired of always confirming yes, you actually do want to empty the Trash, open a Finder window and choose Finder⇨Preferences. Click Advanced in the Preferences window that appears and then remove the check mark next to Show Warning before Emptying the Trash.

Figure 3-13: Dig through the Trash to ensure you didn't throw away anything important.

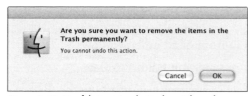

Figure 3-14: Careful! Emptying the Trash can't be undone.

Back Up Files to a CD

1. In the Finder or simply on the Desktop (the menu bar at the top of the screen must say Finder), choose File⇨New Burn Folder.

2. Type a name for the Burn folder. The name will be the disc volume name when the disc is recorded.

3. Click and drag files and folders to the Burn folder.

4. To review the items in the Burn folder, double-click the folder to open it.

5. To find out how much space will be required to store the files in the Burn folder, click the Calculate Burn Folder Space button at the bottom of the Burn Folder window. The space required appears at the bottom of the Burn Folder window, as shown in Figure 3-15.

    The Calculate Burn Folder Space button is round and is located in the lower-right corner of the Burn Folder window. Remember, most CDs can hold 700MB of data and most DVDs hold up to 4.3GB of data. To burn DVDs, your computer must have a SuperDrive or external DVD burner.

6. After you're done adding files, click Burn in the Burn Folder window.

7. When you're prompted to do so, insert a blank recordable disc of the appropriate size.

8. Choose a burn speed, as shown in Figure 3-16, and then click Burn.

    Recording errors are less likely to occur at slower burn speeds. Unless you're in a hurry, choose the slowest burn speed possible.

Figure 3-15: Calculate the space required for your burn.

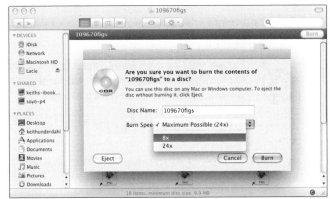

Figure 3-16: Slower burn speeds are more reliable.

Back Up Your Computer with Time Machine

1. If you have an external hard drive, connect it to your computer and prepare it for use, as I describe in Chapter 23.

     An external drive isn't required for using Time Machine, but files that are backed up to an external drive will be safer in case a component inside your computer fails.

2. Open System Preferences and then click the Time Machine icon.

3. Next to Back Up To, click Configure.

4. Select a drive to which you want backups to be saved, as shown in Figure 3-17.

     If storage space is a major concern, place a check mark next to Automatically Delete Backups Older Than and then select a time frame. Shorter time frames use less disk space.

5. Click OK to return to the main Time Machine control panel.

6. If you have a folder containing large files that don't need to be backed up, click the Add button (it looks like a plus sign) under Do Not Back Up and then browse to the desired folder. In Figure 3-18, two items will not be backed up by Time Machine.

7. To start a backup immediately, click Back Up Now and then close the Time Machine control panel. Backups occur silently and don't interfere with your other work.

Figure 3-17: Select a volume to which backups are saved.

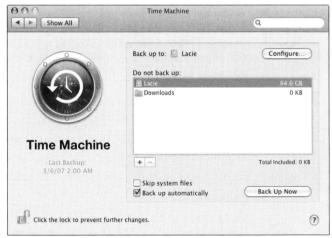

Figure 3-18: You can pick and choose what's backed up by Time Machine.

Restore Files with Time Machine

1. Click the Time Machine icon on the Dock.

2. In the Time Machine window that appears, as shown in Figure 3-19, click the arrows in the lower-right corner of the screen to move to earlier backups.

 You can also click a screen in the main window to jump directly to it. Each screen in the background represents a different backup time. You can also move through backups by clicking the graduated scale along the right side of the Time Machine screen.

3. Use the Finder window and its sidebar to browse to the file that you want to restore. If you can't find the desired file, go back in time to an earlier backup.

4. When you find the file that you want to back up, select it and click Restore in the lower-right corner of the Time Machine window.

 Click Cancel if you want to close Time Machine without restoring a file.

5. Check the restored file to make sure it's the one you want. If the restored file has the same name as an item that's currently on your computer, the restored file assumes the proper name and the existing file has (original) tacked onto its name, as shown in Figure 3-20.

Figure 3-19: Move back in time on your system using Time Machine.

Figure 3-20: Compare current and restored versions after performing a backup.

Suppress Desktop Icons for CDs and iPods

1. Open a Finder window (or click an empty area of the Desktop) and choose Finder⇨Preferences.

2. In General options, remove the check mark next to CDs, DVDs, and iPods, as shown in Figure 3-21.

3. Close the Finder Preferences window.

 You can still eject discs and iPods by using the Eject commands in iTunes and DVD Player by using the Eject key on your keyboard, or by clicking the Eject symbol next to the item in a Finder window sidebar.

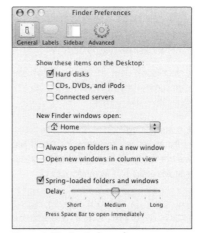

Figure 3-21: Use Finder preferences to suppress certain Desktop icons.

Adjusting System Preferences

The Macintosh computer is known for its ease of use, but "easy" doesn't mean simplistic. Beneath the friendly exterior of OS X is a powerful operating system, which can be configured for almost any task by using a wide selection of hardware.

This chapter shows you how to configure the system software for your specific needs and hardware. Tasks show you how to take command of both the internal hardware in your Mac and the peripherals attached to it. Specific tasks include

➡ **Internal components:** Operating system tools help you make the most efficient use of your laptop's batteries, decide which disk is used to boot the system, and update the OS X software.

➡ **Peripherals:** Your Mac can work with a variety of different printers, monitors, keyboards, and audio devices. Configuring peripherals in OS X is easy.

The tasks in this chapter show you how to control your computer's hardware with OS X software tools. The final task also shows you more about the specifications and performance of your computer, which is important if you decide to make some upgrades. If you want to upgrade the actual hardware of your Mac, see Chapter 23.

Chapter

4

Get ready to . . .

Save Energy with Power Settings

1. Open System Preferences by choosing Apple⇨System Preferences.

2. Click the Energy Saver icon.

3. If you have a laptop, choose Battery in the Settings menu, and then select a power saving profile in the Optimization menu.

4. Click Sleep to display Sleep options, as shown in Figure 4-1.

5. Adjust the sliders to change when the computer and monitor will go to sleep.

 The monitor uses a lot of power, so it's a good idea to let the display sleep after a minute or two of inactivity.

6. Click Options to review power saving options, such as whether you want a Battery icon to appear on the menu bar or whether you want the display to dim automatically before going to sleep.

 The settings available on the Options screen vary depending on whether you're adjusting Power Adapter or Battery settings.

7. Click Schedule. If you want the computer to wake or start at a certain time each day, place a check mark next to Start Up or Wake and then choose dates and times for automatic startup, as shown in Figure 4-2.

8. If you have a laptop, choose Power Adapter in the Settings For menu and then repeat Steps 3-7 to adjust settings for when your computer is plugged in to wall power.

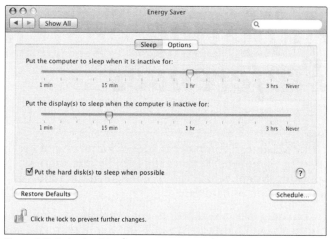

Figure 4-1: During inactivity, the computer can go to sleep to save power.

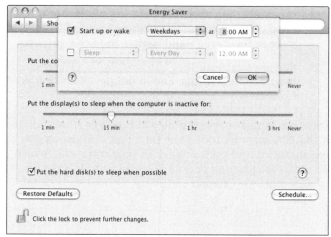

Figure 4-2: Schedule your computer to start up or sleep automatically.

Update System Software

1. Make sure that your computer is connected to the Internet.

2. Close all open applications.

 Look at the Dock and make sure that you quit all programs. Running programs have a small, black triangle below their icons. You can't quit the Finder and Dashboard, but you can quit everything else.

3. Choose Apple⇨Software Update. After a few seconds, a list of available updates appears in the Software Update window.

4. Review each item and remove check marks next to items that you don't want to update, as shown in Figure 4-3.

 If you're not sure what an item is, click it once. A description of the update appears in the bottom section of the Software Update window.

5. Click the Install button at the bottom of the Software Update window to begin downloading the updates.

6. Enter your administrator password when you're prompted to do so, as shown in Figure 4-4, and then click OK.

7. Read and accept any license agreements that appear. If you're downloading multiple updates, you may have to accept multiple agreements. After you accept all the agreements, a status window shows you the download status of your updates.

 When you review the list of updates, look for ones that say they must be installed separately. These should be downloaded individually, which means you may have to run Software Update a couple of times.

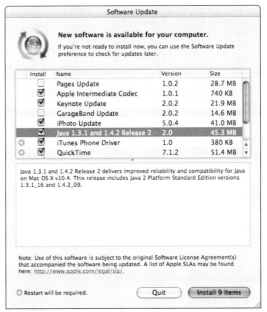

Figure 4-3: Deselect updates for programs or features you don't use.

Figure 4-4: An administrator password is required to install updates.

Select a Startup Disk

1. Open System Preferences and then click the Startup Disk icon.

2. Select the disk you want to use when the computer starts up, as shown in Figure 4-5.

3. If you want to restart the computer right now using a different disk or operating system, click Restart. Otherwise, simply close the Startup Disk window.

Manage Printers

1. Open System Preferences and then click the Print & Fax icon.

2. To add a printer, click the Add button (it looks like a plus sign) below the list of available printers.

3. Click the button corresponding to the type of printer that you want to add. For example, click Windows if you are adding a printer connected to a Windows PC on your network, or Bluetooth to add a Bluetooth printer.

4. Select the name of the computer to which the new printer is connected, as shown in Figure 4-6.

 Normally, it is necessary to manually add network printers only. Printers installed directly to your computer following the printer manufacturer's instructions should already appear in your list of printers.

Figure 4-5: Select the disk or operating system that you want to use when the computer starts.

Figure 4-6: Select the computer to which the new printer is connected.

5. When you're prompted to enter a name and password, enter a username and password that is valid on the computer to which you're trying to connect. Click OK.

6. Select the name of the printer that you want to add, as shown in Figure 4-7.

7. In the Print Using menu, choose Select a Driver to Use, and then choose the model name in the list that appears below. Click Add.

 If your printer's manufacturer or model isn't listed in any menu, choose Generic PostScript Printer in the Print Using menu.

8. In the list of printers, as shown in Figure 4-8, check the status of your newly added printer. A green dot next to the printer's name means that the printer is ready to use.

9. To set a specific printer as your default printer, choose that printer in the Selected Printer in Print Dialog menu, as shown in Figure 4-8.

10. To adjust printer-specific settings, select the printer and click Options & Supplies. The Printer Options and Supplies utility runs, with options and settings tailored to the printer. Here you can change the name and model of the printer, its location, and other details.

Figure 4-7: Select the name of the printer that you want to add.

Figure 4-8: Set a default printer and more in the Print & Fax window.

Calibrate the Display Color

1. Open System Preferences and then click the Displays icon.

2. Click Color to open the color preferences for your monitor.

3. Choose a profile that matches your monitor or display, as shown in Figure 4-9.

     If you're not sure which profile is compatible with your monitor, place a check mark next to Show Profiles for This Display Only. Incompatible profiles disappear from the list.

     Color calibration is usually necessary only if you have special color needs — for example, you're editing video for broadcast or performing professional graphics production — or if you're not satisfied with the color performance of your monitor.

4. Click Calibrate.

5. Read the instructions in the Display Calibrator Assistant and then click Continue.

     Do not use the Expert mode unless your monitor performs poorly and you're experienced with color calibration.

6. Follow the wizard instructions to calibrate colors. When you get to the Select a Target Gamma screen, as shown in Figure 4-10, you may want to choose a setting that matches the target display of your work rather than your computer's current display.

7. On the last screen of the Display Calibrator Assistant, click Done to create your new calibrated color profile.

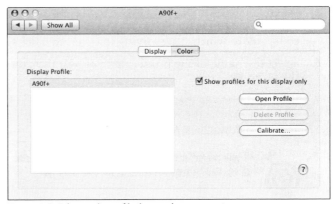

Figure 4-9: Select a color profile that matches your monitor.

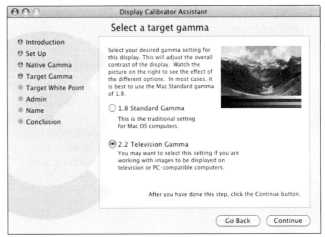

Figure 4-10: Experiment at each step to calibrate your display.

Change Keyboard and Mouse Settings

1. Open System Preferences and then click the Keyboard & Mouse icon.

2. Click the Keyboard button to bring keyboard settings to the front, as shown in Figure 4-11.

3. Adjust the Key Repeat Rate and Delay Until Repeat sliders to change the rate of repeat when you hold down keyboard keys.

> If you have a laptop but want to use the function keys (F1 through F12) for application features, place a check mark next to Use the F1–F12 Keys to Control Software Features.

4. Click the Trackpad or Mouse button, as appropriate.

> If you're using a laptop, the Mouse button appears only if a mouse is connected to the computer.

5. Use the sliders to adjust the tracking speed, double-click speed, and scrolling speed (if appropriate), as shown in Figure 4-12.

6. Adjust other device specific settings, including

   - **Two-button mouse:** If you have a two-button mouse, you can choose whether the right or left button is the primary button.

   - **Trackpads:** Newer Apple trackpads incorporate two-fingered scrolling. You can also enable clicking by tapping on the trackpad.

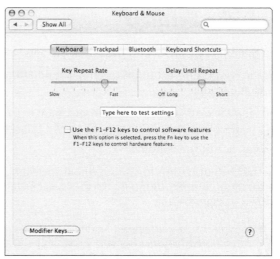

Figure 4-11: Change the keyboard repeat rate here.

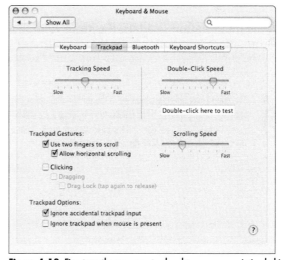

Figure 4-12: Fine-tune the mouse or trackpad to your own pointing habits.

Adjust Audio Settings

1. Open System Preferences and then click the Sound icon.

2. Click the Sound Effects button to bring sound effect settings to the front.

3. Choose a new alert sound, as shown in Figure 4-13.

4. Choose whether you want audible feedback to play when you adjust the volume.

5. Click the Output button to choose which speakers are used for audio output and to adjust the speaker balance, as shown in Figure 4-14.

    In some cases, an operating system bug can cause audio balance to change inadvertently when you adjust volume with the function keys. If your speakers don't seem to be balanced properly between the left and right channels, open the sound output settings and double-check the volume.

6. Click the Input button to adjust the input volume for your computer's microphone. Speak normally and watch the Input Level indicators to fine-tune the microphone level.

    The Input Level indicators light up to the middle and upper part of the scale during speech. If the level is too low, your voice will be too quiet. If the level is too high and the indicators routinely bounce off the top of the scale, audible distortion may occur.

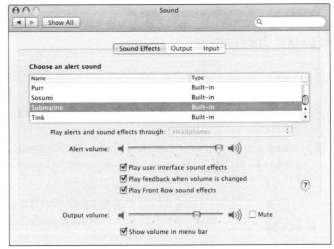

Figure 4-13: You can customize the OS X alert sound.

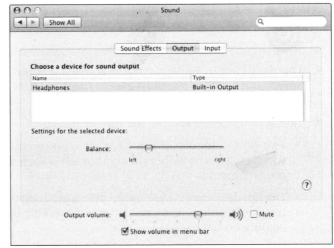

Figure 4-14: Use Output settings to adjust audio balance.

Checking System Specifications and Performance

1. Choose Apple⇨About This Mac, and then click More Info.

2. In the System Profiler window that appears, click Disc Burning in the Hardware menu.

 If you're not sure whether your computer has a Combo drive for burning CDs or a SuperDrive for burning both CDs and DVDs, check the Disc Burning properties. If you see a DVD-Write section, your Mac has a SuperDrive.

3. Click Memory in the Hardware menu to check the size and status of your system memory, as shown in Figure 4-15. The Status column lists the performance status of each memory slot.

4. Click AirPort Card in the Network menu to see what kind of AirPort card (AirPort or AirPort Extreme) you have.

5. Click Applications in the Software menu to list the applications installed on your computer as shown in Figure 4-16. Review the list and note the system listed in the Kind column. Most applications are one of four kinds:

- **Classic:** Requires OS 9 to be installed

- **PowerPC or Native:** Compatible with OS X running on PowerPC-based Macs

- **Intel:** Compatible with OS X running on Intel-based Macs

- **Universal:** Universal binary, compatible with PowerPC- and Intel-based Macs

6. Review other categories as needed.

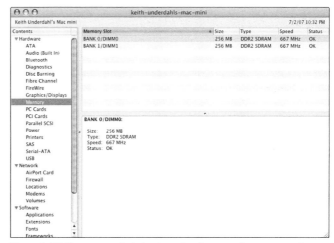

Figure 4-15: Here you can check the size and performance of your computer's memory.

Figure 4-16: Check the system compatibility of your applications.

Part 2
Getting to Work in OS X

Utilizing OS X Applications

Chapter 5

Personal computers first became popular in the 1980s, well before iPods and the Internet became integral parts of our lives. Why did people spend hundreds or even thousands of dollars on computers like the Apple II, TRS-80, IBM PC, and early Macintosh? Even before digital multimedia and the online world, computers served as powerful tools for organizing lives, typing reports and memos, and storing information.

Today we take it for granted that our computers will help us compose letters, track schedules, and manage contacts. And with a Mac, you really *can* take these things for granted because new Macintosh computers come with an array of free programs to help you accomplish many common tasks. These programs live in the OS X Applications folder, and this chapter shows you how to use some of them. This chapter shows you how to

➡ Keep a personal schedule with iCal.

➡ Manage names, addresses, and other contact information with the Address Book.

➡ Edit text files with TextEdit.

➡ Store and organize pictures with iPhoto (a free program on most new Macs, or available as part of iLife).

➡ Expand your vocabulary with the built-in dictionary.

➡ Recover from unfortunate deletions with Time Machine.

➡ Save any file as a PDF file for easy online sharing.

Open the Applications Folder

1. Open any Finder window. You can click the Finder icon on the Dock or simply double-click the hard drive icon on your Desktop.

2. Click Applications in the Finder Sidebar to open the Applications folder, as shown in Figure 5-1.

3. To launch an application, simply double-click its icon in the Applications folder.

 In some cases you may need to open a subfolder before launching an application. For example, if you have Microsoft Office installed, you may need to open the Office subfolder in the Applications folder before opening a program, such as Word or Excel.

Plan Your Life with iCal

1. Open the Applications folder and then double-click the iCal icon.

 You may also be able to launch iCal from the Dock.

2. In the Calendars menu on the left side of the iCal window, place check marks next to the calendars you want to display. For example, if you want only your home schedule to display, remove the check mark next to Work.

3. To create a new calendar (in addition to the default Home and Work calendars), choose File⇨New Calendar and then type a name for the calendar, as shown in Figure 5-2.

4. To add a calendar event, first select the calendar to which it should be added.

Figure 5-1: Applications are easy to find in OS X.

Figure 5-2: iCal lets you keep separate calendars for various parts of your life.

5. In the month calendar shown in the lower-left corner of the iCal screen, click the day on which you want to create the event.

Use the arrows above the calendar to move to a different month.

6. In the main calendar window in the middle of the iCal screen, click and drag a box around the time of your event or appointment and then type a name for the event, as shown in Figure 5-3.

7. For a monthly overview of appointments, click Month near the top of the iCal window.

8. To see details of an event, double-click the event in the main calendar. Information about the event appears in a pop-up Event window, as shown in Figure 5-4.

9. Type notes pertaining to the event in the lower section of the Event window or change the time and other event details in the upper section. Click Done to close the Event window.

If the event is an all-day appointment, place a check mark next to All-Day in the Info pane on the right side of the screen.

Use the Calendar menu in the Info pane to move events from one of your calendars (such as Home) to another calendar (such as Work).

10. To remove an event from iCal, simply click the event once to select it and then press the Delete key on your keyboard.

If you delete an event by accident, you can undo the deletion by choosing Edit⇨Undo.

Figure 5-3: Adding events to the calendar is easy.

Figure 5-4: You can view your calendar by month as well.

Add Contacts to Your Address Book

1. Open the Applications folder and then double-click the Address Book icon to launch the Address Book.

 You can also launch the Address Book from other applications, such as iCal and Apple Mail.

2. To add a new person to the Address Book, click the Add New Person button, which looks like a plus sign and is located below the list of names.

3. Type the person's name, company, phone numbers, addresses, and other information, as shown in Figure 5-5.

4. To edit an entry later, simply click the name of the person you want to change and then click Edit under their Card.

5. To add a picture to a person's Address Book card, click the name in the list and then double-click the picture icon next to the name.

6. In the picture chooser that appears as shown in Figure 5-6, click Choose. Use the Finder window that appears to find and select an image on your hard drive.

7. Zoom in on the image by using the Zoom slider below the picture and then click and drag the image left or right and up or down to reposition it. The area in the central box will be used in the Address Book.

8. Click Set.

9. To remove a person from your Address Book, select the name in the Name list and then choose Edit⇨Delete Card.

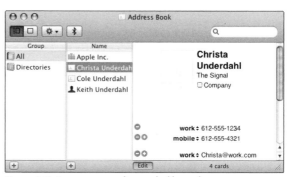

Figure 5-5: Enter names, numbers, and addresses here.

Figure 5-6: You can add personal photos to Address Book cards.

Edit Text with TextEdit

1. Open the Applications folder and then double-click the TextEdit icon.

2. Begin typing text, as shown in Figure 5-7.

3. To change the size or formatting of text, click and drag over a passage of text to select it and then choose Format⇨Font. Make a selection from the Font window to change the size of text or apply characteristics, such as bold or italics.

 You can change alignment and spacing of text by choosing Format⇨Text.

4. To save your work, choose File⇨Save. Choose a folder in which to save the file and enter a name.

5. To print your text, choose File⇨Print. Select a printer, specify the pages to print and the number of copies of each, and then click Print.

6. If you're not happy with the default text size or appearance, choose TextEdit⇨Preferences to open the Preferences window, as shown in Figure 5-8.

7. Choose whether you want the default format to be Rich Text or Plain Text. Rich Text allows you to format text so that it looks nice, but Plain Text is required for certain types of files, such as HyperText Markup Language (HTML) files.

8. To change the default text appearance, click Change next to either Plain Text Font or Rich Text Font. In the Font window, choose different default fonts, styles, and sizes, as desired.

Figure 5-7: TextEdit is a basic, no-frills text editor.

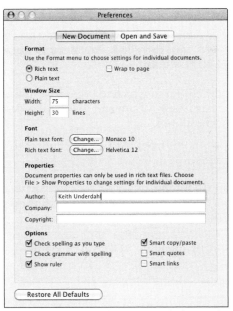

Figure 5-8: Change the default text size and other TextEdit settings here.

Organize Pictures with iPhoto

1. Open the Applications folder and then double-click the iPhoto icon. If you're launching iPhoto for the first time, you're asked if you want to use iPhoto when you connect a digital camera to the computer. Click a button to make a choice.

2. Connect your digital camera to your computer's Universal Serial Bus (USB) port and turn on the camera. The camera should be in picture viewing mode, not picture taking mode.

3. When iPhoto switches to Import mode, as shown in Figure 5-9, type a name and description for the roll.

4. Click Import to begin importing photos from your camera.

     To import pictures that are already on your hard drive into iPhoto, choose File➪Add to Library. Use the Finder window that appears to browse and import photos.

5. To create a new album in which to organize certain pictures, choose File➪New Album and then type a descriptive name for the album.

6. Click and drag photos from the Library window to the new album, as shown in Figure 5-10.

     To copy multiple photos, first click and drag a box around the photos you want to move. After a group is selected, you can click and drag that group to a new album.

7. Click the name of an album to view its contents.

Figure 5-9: iPhoto automatically detects most digital cameras.

Figure 5-10: Click and drag pictures to copy them to different albums.

Create PDF Files

1. Create a document in any application. The document can be text, a picture, or almost anything else, and it can be created in a bundled OS X application or a third-party application.

2. After you're done editing the file, choose Edit⇨Print.

3. Choose PDF⇨Save as PDF, as shown in Figure 5-11.

4. Type a file name for the PDF file in the Save as field.

5. Choose a location in which to save the PDF file in the Where menu.

6. Click Save.

7. Locate the saved PDF file and double-click it to open it. If you have a PDF reader program, such as Adobe Reader installed, the PDF file opens in that program, as shown in Figure 5-12. Otherwise, the PDF file opens in Preview.

 If you don't have Adobe Reader installed on your computer, visit www.adobe.com to download it for free. Although the OS X Preview program can open and display PDFs, Preview can't take full advantage of PDF features such as cross-document links, forms, and multi-volume searching.

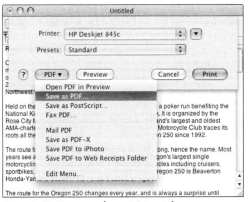

Figure 5-11: Use any application's Print window to create a PDF file.

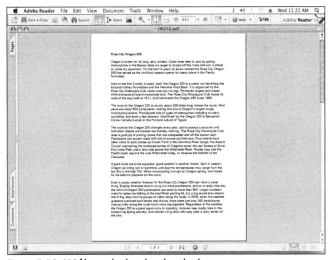

Figure 5-12: PDF files can be shared easily with others.

Look Up Words in the Dictionary

1. Open the Applications folder and then double-click the Dictionary icon.

2. Start typing a word in the search box of the Dictionary and Thesaurus window, as shown in Figure 5-13. Type slowly and note the list of words that appears and is narrowed down with each letter you add. If the word you type isn't in the dictionary, you see a warning and suggestions, as shown in Figure 5-13.

3. Double-click a word in the list to view its definition, as shown in Figure 5-14.

4. Scroll down the page to find derivatives, etymology, and synonyms.

5. To return to the previous Dictionary screen, choose History➪Back.

 The Dictionary is interactive. If you see a word in a definition that you don't understand, simply double-click the word. That word's Dictionary entry appears.

 To change the preferred Dictionary or pronunciation guide, choose Dictionary➪Preferences. In the Preferences window, you can change these and other Dictionary settings.

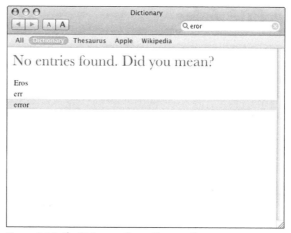

Figure 5-13: The Dictionary tells you if your spelling is incorrect.

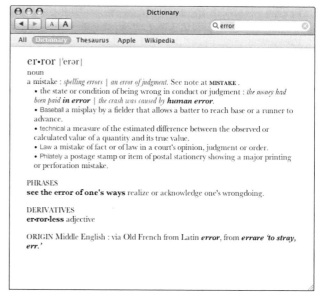

Figure 5-14: The Dictionary lists definitions and synonyms.

Quit an Application

1. To see if an application is still running, hover the mouse pointer over the Dock. Icons with arrows below them — such as TextEdit and Preview, as shown in Figure 5-15 — are still running, even if you closed all documents in that program.

2. To quit an application, first click the application's icon on the Dock to make the application active.

3. Click the name of the application (for example, TextEdit or Preview) on the menu bar and choose Quit from the menu that appears, as shown in Figure 5-16.

You can also press ⌘+Q to quickly quit an active program.

Make a habit of quitting programs after you're done using them. Each program that is left running uses up some memory and other system resources. Unlike Windows programs, most Macintosh applications don't quit when you simply click a window's red Close button.

Figure 5-15: An arrow below the icon means that program is still running.

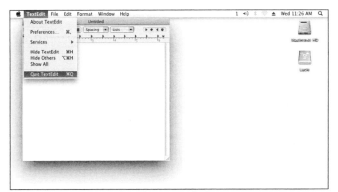

Figure 5-16: You must quit the application to truly close it.

Using Productivity Software

Y ou may have heard some of your Windows-using friends say things like, "I'd use a Mac, but the programs I need aren't available for OS X."

Given this perception, it comes as a surprise to many people that, in fact, a lot of applications *are* available for OS X, including ubiquitous Microsoft Office applications like Word, PowerPoint, and Excel. If you have work to get done, your Macintosh is up to the task.

Applications, such as word processors, spreadsheet programs, and presentation programs, are often called *productivity* programs. Apple offers its own suite of productivity programs — *iWork*. iWork is more affordable than Microsoft Office and includes *Pages* (a word processor) and *Keynote* (a presentation program).

This chapter focuses primarily on iWork applications although many of the basic techniques apply to Microsoft Office as well. To order iWork, visit your local Apple retailer or see www.apple.com/iwork. Tasks show how to create and edit new presentations and word processing documents with iWork applications.

 Free trials of Apple iWork and Microsoft Office are pre-installed in the Applications folders of most new Macs. For more on using Microsoft Office applications for OS X, check out *Microsoft Office v.10 for Macs For Dummies* by Tom Negrino (Wiley Publishing, Inc.).

Chapter
6

Get ready to . . .

Create a New Pages Document

1. Launch Pages from the iWork subfolder in the Applications folder.

    If this is your first time launching iWork, click Try to test iWork free for 30 days.

2. Choose a template for your new document, as shown in Figure 6-1. To choose a template, click a document category in the list on the left and then scroll through the available templates on the right. When you find the template you want to use, click the template to select it and then click Choose.

    To create another new document at any time in Pages, choose File⇨New.

3. Begin typing text, as you would in any word processor or text editing program.

4. To save the document, choose File⇨Save.

5. In the Save As sheet that appears, type a name for the document. If you want to choose a different folder, click the down arrow to the right of the Save As field to open a small Finder window, as shown in Figure 6-2.

6. After you give a name and select the folder that you want to save the file in, click Save.

    Save your document frequently while you work. To quickly save a document, press ⌘+S.

Figure 6-1: Pages includes many helpful document templates.

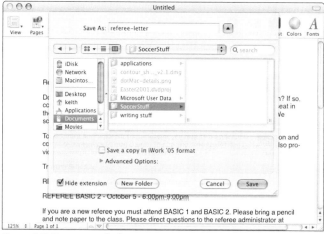

Figure 6-2: Save your work often.

Style Text in Pages

1. Click to place the cursor in the paragraph to which you want to apply a paragraph style.

2. Click the Style menu and choose a paragraph style, as shown in Figure 6-3.

3. To change the alignment of text, place the cursor in the desired paragraph and choose Format⇨Text. Choose an alignment option, such as Center or Justify.

4. To create a bulleted or numbered list, select each line of text in the list and then click the List button. Choose a list style from the submenu that appears.

5. To change the style of a smaller passage of text, click and drag over the text to select it, as shown in Figure 6-4.

6. Click the Fonts button on the far-right side of the Pages toolbar and then choose a different font or style. The Fonts panel organizes fonts into collections and families. In Figure 6-4, the selected text was made bold.

You can also access font properties and other appearance settings by choosing Format⇨Font.

To change the color of selected text, click and drag to select the text and then click the Colors button. Use the Colors panel that appears to choose a new text color.

7. Close the Font window after you're done changing the text.

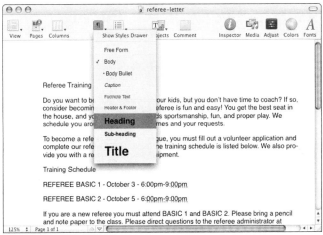

Figure 6-3: Quickly style text by using paragraph styles.

Figure 6-4: Click and drag over text to select it.

Insert a Photo into a Pages Document

1. Create a document, into which you want to insert a photo, in Pages.

2. Place the cursor where you want to insert the photo.

3. Choose Insert⇨Choose.

4. Browse to the photo you want to insert.

5. Click the photo to select it, as shown in Figure 6-5, and then click Insert to include it in the document.

 If the image doesn't fit well into your document, click and drag the corner handles of the image to resize it.

Print a Pages Document

1. Compose a document in Pages, as I describe earlier in this chapter.

2. Choose File⇨Print.

3. In the Print tab that appears, click the down arrow to expand print options, as shown in Figure 6-6.

4. Select the number of copies and other print options, as shown in Figure 6-6.

5. Click Print to begin printing.

 To create a PDF file of your document, choose PDF⇨Save as PDF in the lower-left corner of the Print window.

Figure 6-5: Choose the photo that you want to insert.

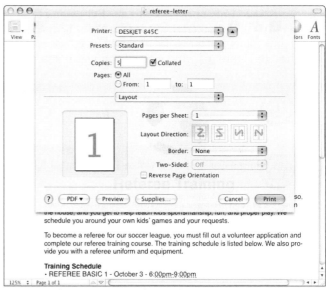

Figure 6-6: Choose printing options for your document.

Start a New Keynote Presentation

1. Open the iWork subfolder in the Applications folder and then double-click Keynote to launch the program.

    If this is your first time launching iWork, click Try to test iWork free for 30 days.

2. Choose a template, as shown in Figure 6-7, for your new presentation. To choose a template, scroll through the list of available templates on the right. When you find the template you want to use, click the template to select it.

3. Select a size for your slides in the Slide Size menu.

    If your presentation will be viewed in a large room via a projector with average lighting and resolution, stick with a relatively small slide size, such as 800 x 600. Larger slide sizes may result in text that is hard to read from the back row.

4. Click Choose to create a new presentation by using your chosen template and slide size.

5. Type a title and subtitle for your presentation in the provided text boxes on the first slide.

6. Choose File⊏⊃Save.

7. In the Save tab that appears, enter a file name for your presentation, as shown in Figure 6-8.

8. Choose a folder in which to save the presentation in the Where menu and then click Save.

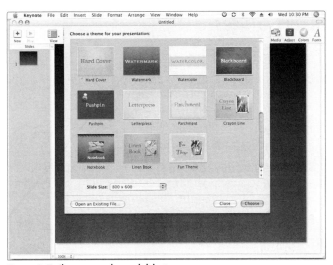

Figure 6-7: Choose a template and slide size.

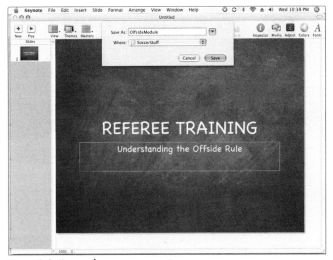

Figure 6-8: Name and save your presentation.

Insert Slides

1. Open a Keynote presentation.

2. Click the New button in the upper-left corner of the Keynote window to insert a new slide, as shown in Figure 6-9.

3. To open a specific slide, click the slide in the Slides list on the left side of the screen.

4. To change the order of slides, click and drag slides up or down to new positions. Slides at the top of the list appear first when the slideshow is played.

5. To quickly change the layout or format of a slide, click the Masters button and choose a new master, as shown in Figure 6-10.

6. Click in the text areas and type text for your new slide.

 To delete a slide, open the slide and choose Edit⇨Delete. If you have a two-button mouse, you can also right-click a slide and choose Delete from the contextual menu that appears.

 To quickly create a new slide based on an existing slide, open the existing slide and choose Edit⇨Duplicate. An exact copy of the slide is added to the presentation.

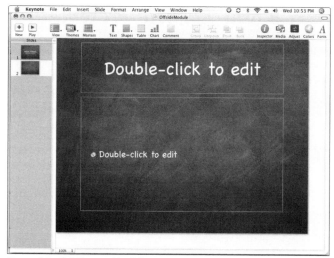

Figure 6-9: Click New to add a slide.

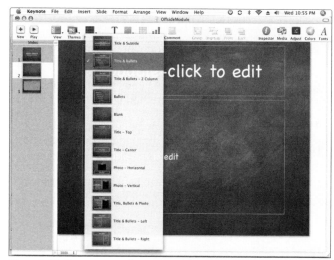

Figure 6-10: Choose a master for your new slide.

Formatting Text

1. Enter text into a text box on a slide.

    To add a new text box to a slide, click the Text button on the Keynote toolbar. Click and drag the text box to the desired location and resize the box by using the handles on the sides and corners.

2. Click and drag over a passage of text to select it.

3. To change the size or style of the text, click the Fonts button on the Keynote toolbar.

4. Select a font, style, and size, as shown in Figure 6-11.

    To add a drop shadow behind the selected text, click the Drop Shadow button. (The button is rectangular, located in the upper-middle section of the Font panel, and is marked with the letter T.)

5. Close the Font panel after you're done customizing the font.

6. To change the color of text (or any object), select the text and then click the Colors button on the Keynote toolbar.

7. Use the Colors panel, as shown in Figure 6-12, to select a new color.

    If you prefer to adjust color with sliders or specific numeric values rather than the circular color picker, click the Sliders button (the second button from the left) near the top of the Colors panel.

8. Close the Colors panel after you're done changing colors.

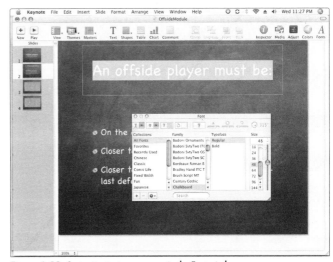

Figure 6-11: Customize text appearance in the Font window.

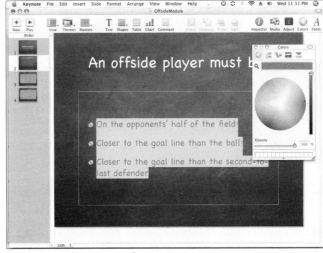

Figure 6-12: Colors are easy to change in Keynote.

Add Graphics to Presentations

1. Open a Keynote presentation and a slide on which you want to draw some basic graphics.

2. Click the Shapes button, as shown in Figure 6-13, and choose a shape that you want to draw.

3. When the shape appears on the screen, click and drag the corner and side handles to change the shape size.

4. To insert a photo, choose Insert⇨Choose.

5. Browse to the image file that you want to insert. Select the image file and then click Insert.

6. Click and drag the image to a new location, as shown in Figure 6-14.

7. Click and drag the corner handles of the image to resize it.

 Don't make pictures too small because the people sitting in the back row must be able to see them, too.

8. If a shape or image blocks part of another image or object, select the image and choose Arrange⇨Bring Forward or Arrange⇨Send Backwards, as appropriate. Repeat until all graphics and objects on the slide are stacked in the proper order.

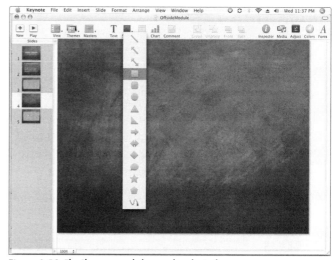

Figure 6-13: The Shapes menu helps you draw basic shapes.

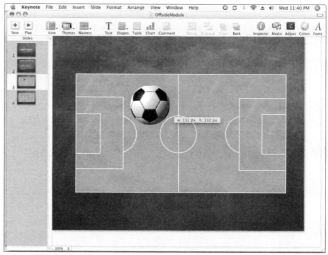

Figure 6-14: Photos can be used to enhance your presentation.

Present a Keynote Presentation

1. Connect your Mac to a projector, if needed.

     You may need to use a special VGA adapter between your Mac and the projector cable. Apple offers VGA adapters that allow you to connect most Macs to analog computer monitors or multimedia projectors.

2. Open the presentation that you want to play in Keynote.

3. Click the first slide in the presentation so that it is selected.

4. Click the Play button or choose View⇨Play Slideshow to play the slideshow, as shown in Figure 6-15.

5. Press Return, the spacebar, the right arrow key, or the mouse button to move to the next slide.

6. To move to the previous slide, press the left arrow key.

7. To end the presentation, press the Esc key.

8. To export the presentation in a different format, choose File⇨Export.

9. In the Export tab that appears, as shown in Figure 6-16, choose an export format and follow the instructions onscreen to export the presentation. The most useful formats include

    *   **QuickTime:** Plays on any computer with QuickTime

    *   **PowerPoint:** Exports a presentation that is compatible with Microsoft PowerPoint

    *   **Flash:** Plays in most Web browsers

    *   **iDVD:** Creates a DVD that can play in many video DVD players

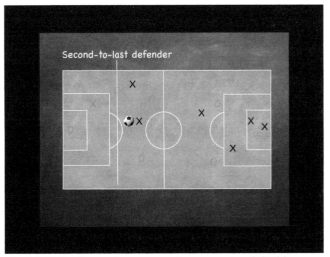

Figure 6-15: Use the mouse button or arrow keys to move through the slides.

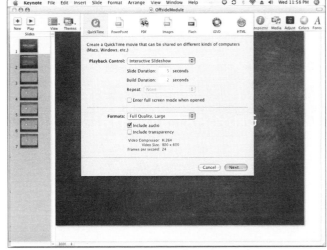

Figure 6-16: Keynote can export presentations for QuickTime and PowerPoint.

Using Dashboard

Computers are said to be labor saving devices, yet it seems to take an awful lot of mouse clicks, menu commands, and keyboard inputs to get anything done. This is what makes computers less intuitive than, say, a car, where every important control is immediately at hand and critical information is within your peripheral view.

The engineers at Apple must have been thinking about computer usability problems, too. When they released OS X version 10.4 Tiger, they included a new tool — *Dashboard.* Like the instrument panel in your car, the OS X Dashboard puts key information and tools within easy reach. Dashboard isn't quite in peripheral view — if it was it would be in the way — but it is just a single mouse click away, and Dashboard doesn't affect your other applications.

This chapter shows you how to open Dashboard and how to add and remove Dashboard items, which are also called *widgets.* Dashboard widgets covered in this chapter include

➠ Weather

➠ Sticky Notes

➠ Web Clips

➠ Flight Tracker

➠ Translation

➠ Unit Converter

➠ Movies

New in OS X Leopard is the ability to easily create your own widgets. The Photocast widget described in this chapter is one such build-your-own Dashboard widget.

Get ready to . . .

Open Dashboard

1. To open Dashboard, simply click the Dashboard button on the Dock. The screen dims slightly, and Dashboard widgets zoom into view, as shown in Figure 7-1. Dashboard can also be opened by two additional methods:

   • Double-click the Dashboard icon in the Applications folder.

   • Press F12 on your keyboard.

2. To change the way Dashboard opens, open System Preferences and then click the Exposé & Spaces icon.

3. To create a hot corner for Dashboard, select Dashboard in one of the Active Screen Corner menus. In Figure 7-2, the lower-right corner has been set to Dashboard. To open Dashboard, simply move the mouse pointer to the corresponding corner of the screen.

4. To change the keyboard shortcut used for opening Dashboard, make a different selection in the Dashboard menu.

 If you want to use a modifier key, such as ⌘ or Control, simply hold down that key (or keys) while making a selection in the Dashboard menu.

 Dashboard can't be quit like other OS X applications. To close Dashboard, simply click a blank area of the screen. Although a black arrow remains under the Dashboard icon on the Dock, very little of your computer's resources are dedicated to Dashboard.

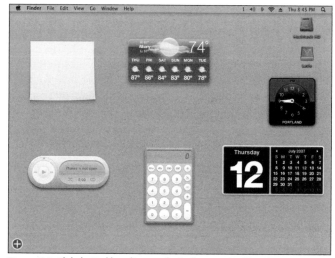

Figure 7-1: Click the Dashboard icon on the Dock to open Dashboard.

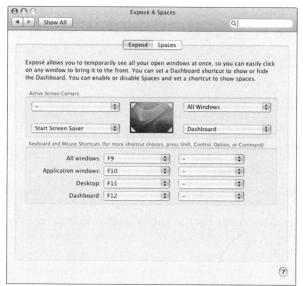

Figure 7-2: Set a hot corner and function key for launching Dashboard.

Add Items to Dashboard

1. Open Dashboard.

2. Click the plus sign in the lower-left corner of the Dashboard screen. A list of widgets appears along the bottom of the screen, as shown in Figure 7-3.

3. Click the arrow buttons on the far right or left of the list of widgets to scroll through the list.

4. To add a widget, simply click the widget in the list. The new widget is plopped onto your Dashboard. In Figure 7-4, the Movies widget was added.

5. Click and drag widgets to move them to new locations, as shown in Figure 7-4.

6. To remove a widget from Dashboard, click the X button in the upper-left corner of the widget. You can always add the widget back later if you want.

7. After you're done adding, moving, and removing widgets, click the X button in the lower-left corner of the screen, just above the horizontal list of widgets. The list disappears, and the X turns back into a plus sign.

 You can click and drag widgets to new locations at any time; the widget list at the bottom of the screen need not be visible when moving widgets, only when adding and removing widgets.

Figure 7-3: Click the plus sign in the lower-left corner to display the widget list.

Figure 7-4: Widgets can be moved or deleted as needed.

Create Web Clip Widgets

1. Open a Web page in Safari containing the item you want to place in a widget.

2. When the page is loaded, choose File⇨Open in Dashboard.

    You can also click the Open This Page in Dashboard button on the Safari toolbar. The button looks like a dotted square with scissors. However, if the item is in a pop-up window, the Safari toolbar may not be visible, making it necessary to choose File⇨Open in Dashboard.

3. Click the general area of the page containing the item that you want to add to Dashboard. A clear box appears around the area.

4. Click and drag the handles at the corners and sides of the box so that the box surrounds only the area that you want to add to Dashboard. In Figure 7-5, I'm selecting a picture and some text in a pop-up window.

5. Click Add. A Web Clip containing the area is added to Dashboard.

6. Open Dashboard and reposition the Web Clip, as shown in Figure 7-6.

7. To remove a Web Clip from your Dashboard, open Dashboard and then click the plus sign in the lower-left corner of the screen. Click the Web Clip's close button to remove it.

Figure 7-5: Select the area that you want to add to Dashboard.

Figure 7-6: Web clips can be moved or closed like any other Dashboard widget.

Check Weather

1. Open Dashboard. If the Weather widget isn't already part of your Dashboard, add it, as described earlier in this chapter.

2. Click the *i* button in the lower-right corner of the Weather widget.

3. In the City, State, or ZIP Code field, enter your city, state, or ZIP code, as shown in Figure 7-7.

 If you live in a suburb of a larger city, make sure you enter the name of your suburb and not the big city nearby. For example, if you live in Aurora, Colorado, enter Aurora and not Denver. This ensures that your weather report is as accurate as possible for your specific location.

4. Choose whether you want the temperature to display in Celsius (°C) or Fahrenheit (°F) in the Degrees menu.

5. If you want the weather outlook to display daily low temperatures as well as daily highs, select Include Lows in 6-Day Forecast.

6. Click Done and then check your weather outlook, as shown in Figure 7-8.

7. For a compact display of the Weather widget, click the sun or moon (depending on the time of day). The widget display gets smaller, like the upper widget in Figure 7-8. Click the sun or moon again to expand the display, like the lower widget in Figure 7-8.

 If you want to monitor the weather in multiple locations, open multiple occurrences of the Weather widget by simply adding the Weather widget again, as described earlier in this chapter. You can then set each widget to a different geographic location.

Figure 7-7: Set your location as specifically as possible.

Figure 7-8: Weather is one of Dashboard's more useful widgets.

Leave Sticky Notes

1. Open Dashboard. If the Stickies widget isn't already part of your Dashboard, add it, as described earlier in this chapter.

2. Click the *i* button in the lower-right corner of the Stickies widget.

3. Choose a paper color, font, and font size, as shown in Figure 7-9.

 For best results, keep the Font Size menu set to Auto. When the size is set to auto, the text side adjusts automatically when you type notes.

4. Click Done.

5. To compose a note, simply click the Stickies widget and start typing, as shown in Figure 7-10.

6. To delete the text on a note, click and drag over text with the mouse to select it and then press Delete on your keyboard.

 If you want to save text in a Sticky Note, select the text and then press ⌘+C on the keyboard to copy it. Open another program (such as TextEdit) and then press ⌘+V to paste the text into that program. You can then save the text with that program. You can't save text by using the Stickies widget.

Figure 7-9: Customize the paper color and font.

Figure 7-10: Type quick notes with the Stickies widget.

Track Flights

1. Open Dashboard. If the Flight Tracker widget isn't already part of your Dashboard, add it, as described earlier in this chapter.

2. If you want to track flights for a specific airline, choose the airline in the Airline menu.

3. Select the departure city in the Depart City menu, as shown in Figure 7-11.

4. Select the destination in the Arrive City menu, as shown in Figure 7-11.

     If you know the three letter airport code (for example, LAX for Los Angeles International Airport or MSP for Minneapolis-St. Paul International Airport) for either city, click in the relevant menu and type the code.

5. Click Find Flights.

6. Review the list of flights matching your results, as shown in Figure 7-12.

7. To perform another search, click the arrow next to the Find Flights button.

     Flight Tracker automatically refreshes its data every time you open Dashboard. If you plan to track a flight in the near future, set up Flight Tracker to monitor those flights beforehand.

Figure 7-11: Enter the arrival and departure cities, and specify an airline if desired.

Figure 7-12: Flight Tracker gives up-to-the-minute flight status.

Translate Foreign Languages

1. Open Dashboard. If the Translation widget isn't already part of your Dashboard, add it, as described earlier in this chapter.

2. Select languages in the From and To menus to decide how the translation is made.

3. Enter a phrase, including punctuation, in the From field. A translation appears automatically in the To field, as shown in Figure 7-13.

 You can copy and paste text into the Translation widget from other programs or Web pages.

Convert Units of Measure

1. Open Dashboard. If the Unit Converter widget isn't already part of your Dashboard, add it, as described earlier in this chapter.

2. Choose a unit you want to convert in the Convert menu. You can choose Weight, Volume, Energy, Currency, Time, and many other units of measure.

3. Select a specific unit of measure in the menu on the left and then enter a value, as shown in Figure 7-14.

4. Choose a specific unit of measure in the right menu. This unit should be the one to which you want to convert the original value.

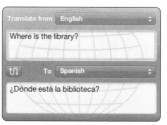

Figure 7-13: Quickly translate phrases to other common languages.

Figure 7-14: The Unit Converter can convert almost anything.

Check Movie Times

1. Open Dashboard. If the Movies widget isn't already part of your Dashboard, add it, as I describe earlier in this chapter.

2. Click in the Movies widget to enlarge the window size.

3. Click the *i* icon in the lower-left corner of the Movies widget and enter your ZIP code, as shown in Figure 7-15.

4. Click Done to return to the main Movies window.

5. Click the name of a movie under Movie Theaters to view a description of the movie. A list of local theaters that are showing the movie appears to the right.

6. Click a theater in the list to view a list of show times, as shown in Figure 7-16.

7. To view a trailer for the movie, click the Trailer icon in the lower-left corner.

8. To purchase tickets online using Fandango.com, click Buy Tickets in the lower-left corner.

 By default, all movies and show times are displayed for the current day. To view a different day, click Today in the upper-right corner of the Movies widget and choose a different day from the menu that appears.

Figure 7-15: Localize the Movies widget for your area.

Figure 7-16: Check movie descriptions, theaters, and show times.

Download New Dashboard Widgets

1. Open Dashboard and then click the plus sign in the lower-left corner to open the list of widgets along the bottom of the screen.

2. Click Manage Widgets in the lower-left corner, just above the widget list.

3. In the Widget Manager window that appears, as shown in Figure 7-17, click More Widgets.

4. In the Apple Web site that appears, as shown in Figure 7-18, browse the extensive list of available widgets.

Figure 7-17: Click More Widgets to see what's available.

 Make sure you read the terms of use for any widget before you download. Widgets listed as Freeware can be downloaded for free, but you should still click the More Info link if one is available. The More Info link also usually contains special installation instructions.

5. After you find a widget you want to install, click Download.

6. Click OK to save the widget to your desktop.

7. After the download is complete, double-click the extracted Widget file to install the widget. Follow the onscreen instructions (unique to each widget) to finish installation.

Figure 7-18: Apple's Web site offers literally thousands of widgets.

Part 3
Going Online with Your Mac

Sending E-Mail and Browsing the Internet

*P*ersonal computers have been available since the 1970s, but in the early years they were mainly used by businesses, gamers, and hardcore computer geeks. With the advent of the World Wide Web in the 1990s, more people came to see personal computers as necessities. Today the computer is an indispensable tool for communication, information, and entertainment.

Your Macintosh is ready to communicate, entertain, and retrieve information as soon as you take it out of the box. It comes with all the software applications you need to send and receive e-mail, browse the Web, or download multimedia. Your Mac probably even comes with the hardware needed to connect to the Internet in the form of a network adapter and AirPort (AirPort is optional on some models). If you need a modem for dial-up Internet, Apple sells one that plugs into your Mac's USB port.

This chapter shows you how to get started with e-mail and Web browsing. In addition to the applications that come with OS X, this chapter also shows you how to download and use *Firefox*, a popular third-party Web browser application.

 Before you can use e-mail and the Internet, you must have an Internet service account. These accounts are provided by Internet Service Providers (ISPs), of which many are probably in your area. If you don't already have Internet service, check with your telephone or cable company to see what services they offer or look in the phone book under Internet Service. Your ISP may provide specific instructions for connecting its service.

Go Online with Safari

1. Launch the Safari Web browser by clicking the Safari icon on the Dock or by double-clicking its icon in the Applications folder.

2. Type a Web address — a *Uniform Resource Locator* (URL) — in the address bar, as shown in Figure 8-1, and then press Return to visit the address.

3. Use the four buttons on the Safari toolbar to navigate Web pages. From left-to-right the buttons are

    *   **Back:** Click the Back button to return to the previously-viewed Web page.

    *   **Forward:** If you click the Back button, you can click the Forward button to return forward.

    *   **Reload:** Use this button to reload a page. The Reload button is especially helpful if a wireless connection drops momentarily and the page fails to completely load.

    *   **Bookmark:** Click this to bookmark a Web page. You can easily return to the page again by selecting it from the Bookmarks menu on the menu bar.

4. To add a bookmark to the Bookmark bar (located just below the Safari toolbar and address bar), go to the page you want to bookmark and then click the Bookmark button.

5. Type a different name for the bookmark, if desired. The name shown appears on the bookmark.

6. Choose Bookmarks Bar in the location menu, as shown in Figure 8-2, and then click Add.

7. To change the size of text on the screen, open the View menu and choose to make text either bigger or smaller.

Figure 8-1: The Safari Web browser comes pre-installed on every Mac.

Figure 8-2: Bookmark pages that you want to visit regularly.

8. Choose Safari➪Preferences.

9. On the General pane, enter the URL for the page you want to use as your home page, as shown in Figure 8-3.

 The *home page* is the Web page that opens when you first launch Safari. To use the current Web page as your home page, click Set to Current Page.

10. Click the Security button to open Security preferences.

11. Choose Never under Cookies if you don't want to accept cookies from Web sites.

12. Close the Preferences window after you're done adjusting Safari preferences.

 Although cookies may be used to track your Web browsing habits, the real risks are minimal. Some Web pages may not function correctly when cookies are disabled.

13. To browse anonymously, choose Safari➪Private Browsing.

 Private browsing stops Safari from remembering which Web pages you've visited. This setting is especially valuable if you're using Safari on a public computer, such as in a library or school.

14. To return to a Web page in History, choose a page from the History menu, or click the Bookmarks button on the far-left side of the Bookmarks bar and then choose History, as shown in Figure 8-4. Click a page in the History to view it.

15. To clear the history, choose History➪Clear History.

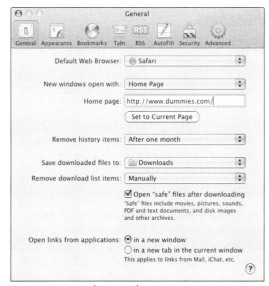

Figure 8-3: Set your home page here.

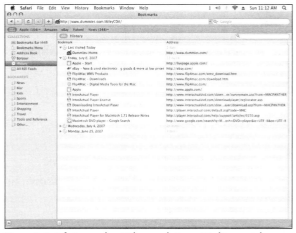

Figure 8-4: Safari remembers Web pages that you visited in recent days.

Install Firefox

1. Use any Web browser (like Safari) to visit www. getfirefox.com.

2. Follow the instructions on the Mozilla Web site to download Firefox.

3. When the installer download is finished, double-click the Desktop icon for the disk image (the icon has the .dmg file name extension) to extract and mount the disk image.

4. Read and accept the license agreement when it appears.

5. When you see the Firefox application window, as shown in the upper-left corner of Figure 8-5, open your Applications folder and then click and drag the Firefox icon from the Firefox window to the Applications folder.

Figure 8-5: Copy Firefox into your Applications folder.

 After Firefox is copied to the Applications folder, you can delete the downloaded Firefox disk image.

 To access Firefox more easily, add it to the OS X Dock. See Chapter 1 for more on adding items to the Dock.

Browse the Web with Firefox

1. Launch Firefox from the Applications folder.

2. Type a Web address in the address bar, as shown in Figure 8-6.

Figure 8-6: Type a URL in the address bar to visit a Web site.

3. Use the navigation buttons on the Firefox toolbar to browse Web pages. From left-to-right the buttons are

- **Back:** Click the Back button to return to the previously-viewed Web page.

- **Forward:** If you click the Back button, you can click the Forward button to return forward.

- **Reload:** Use this button to reload a page. The Reload button is especially helpful if a wireless connection drops momentarily and the page fails to load completely.

- **Stop:** Click this button to stop loading the current Web page.

- **Home:** Click the Home button to quickly return to your home page.

 Click and hold the Back and Forward buttons to reveal a longer list of visited pages.

4. Choose Firefox➪Preferences.

5. In the Main tab, enter the URL for your desired home page, as shown in Figure 8-7, or click Use Current Page to set the current Web page as your home page.

6. Click Check Now to see if Firefox is your default browser. If not, you may set Firefox as the default when you're prompted to do so.

7. To view your browsing history, choose Go➪History. Use the History pane on the left side of the Firefox window, as shown in Figure 8-8, to browse previously visited Web sites.

Figure 8-7: Set Firefox's home page.

Figure 8-8: Choose Go➪History to open the History pane.

Bookmark Your Favorite Web Pages

1. In Firefox, open the Web page that you want to bookmark.

2. Choose Bookmarks⇨Bookmark This Page.

3. Type a simple name for the bookmark in the Bookmark tab that appears, as shown in Figure 8-9.

4. If you want the bookmark to appear on the Bookmarks toolbar, choose Bookmarks Toolbar in the Create In menu, as shown in Figure 8-9.

 To delete or update old bookmarks, choose Bookmarks⇨Manage Bookmarks.

Search with the Google Widget

1. Add the Google widget to Dashboard, as I describe in Chapter 7.

2. Open Dashboard and type a search query in the Google widget, as shown in Figure 8-10.

3. Press Return to begin the search. Your default Web browser opens and displays a list of results.

 Your Web browser doesn't need to be open before you use the Google widget. The browser launches automatically when you begin the search.

Figure 8-9: Bookmark your favorite Web pages in seconds.

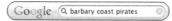

Figure 8-10: Use the Google widget to perform fast Web searches.

Configure an E-Mail Account

1. Obtain an e-mail account from your ISP, an e-mail account provider, or .Mac. See Chapter 9 for more on getting and using a .Mac account.

2. Launch Mail from the OS X Dock or from the Applications folder. Make sure your computer is connected to the Internet.

3. If you have a .Mac e-mail account, enter your .Mac account name and password when you're prompted to do so. If you have a different e-mail account, choose Mail⇨Preferences.

4. Click the Accounts icon in Mail Preferences and then click the Create an Account button (it looks like a plus sign) in the lower-left corner of the Preferences window.

5. Enter your name, e-mail address, and password and then click Continue.

6. Choose the account type and enter the incoming server address (these should be provided with your e-mail account details). Also provide a description and server password, as shown in Figure 8-11.

7. Click Continue and then choose whether your server requires SSL authentication. Click Continue again.

8. Enter the address for your outgoing mail server. If the server requires authentication, check Use Authentication and enter the username and password, as shown in Figure 8-12.

9. Click Continue, verify the account summary that appears, and then click Continue again. Click Done when you see the Conclusion screen.

 If Mail is unable to verify or create the account because you enter an invalid address, username, or password, you're asked to repeat the necessary steps. Addresses, usernames, and passwords are provided by the e-mail service provider.

Figure 8-11: Choose the type of mail account you wish to create.

Figure 8-12: Some outgoing mail servers require authentication.

Compose and Send E-Mail

1. Open the Mail application and click the New Message button on the toolbar.

2. In the message window that appears, type the e-mail address of the recipient in the To: field. If you aren't sure of the address, click Address and choose a name from your Address Book, as shown in Figure 8-13.

 When you receive an e-mail message, you can add the sender to your Address Book by selecting the message and choosing Message⇨Add Sender to Address Book.

3. Type a subject for your message in the Subject: field. The subject should be descriptive so that the recipient can easily identify the topic of your e-mail.

4. Compose your message, as shown in Figure 8-14. The mail composition window works much like a word processor. Other composition options include

    *   **Text styles:** Use the Fonts and Colors buttons to change the appearance of text in your e-mail.

    *   **Carbon copies:** To include a third party in on your e-mail, enter another address in the Cc: field. You can enter multiple addresses in the To: and Cc: fields.

    *   **File attachments:** Click Attach and browse to a picture or other file that you want to send with the e-mail. Try to keep attachment sizes small (usually 1MB or less) and keep in mind that some people can't receive attachments.

5. After you're done composing, click Send. The message is sent.

Figure 8-13: Look up e-mail addresses in your Address Book.

Figure 8-14: Click Send after you're done composing your e-mail.

Download and Read E-Mail

1. Launch Mail and make sure your computer is connected to the Internet.

2. If mail doesn't download automatically, click the Get Mail button on the Mail toolbar.

3. Review the list of downloaded e-mail in the Inbox. Unread e-mail is marked with a blue dot to the left of the message.

4. Click a message to view it in the Preview pane near the bottom of the window, as shown in Figure 8-15.

   To view an e-mail message in a separate window, double-click the message in the Inbox.

5. After you're done reading an e-mail message, you can do one of several things with it:

   • **Reply:** Select a message and click Reply to compose and send a reply to the message.

   • **Delete:** Click the Delete button on the toolbar to delete the message.

   • **Junk:** If the message is spam or junk mail, select the message and click Junk. This trains Mail to recognize and trash junk mail.

   • **Organize:** To organize e-mails that you want to keep, choose Mailbox⇨New Mailbox, type a name for the mailbox, and click OK. Click and drag messages to the new mailbox, as shown in Figure 8-16.

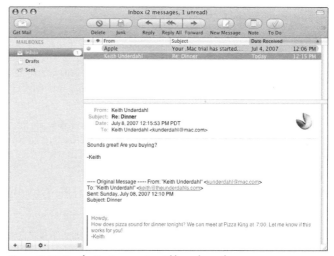

Figure 8-15: Use the Preview pane to quickly read e-mail.

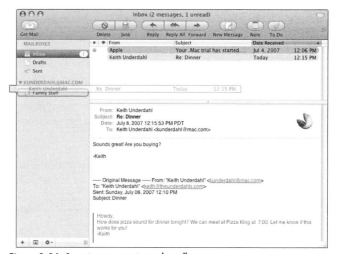

Figure 8-16: Organize messages into sub-mailboxes.

Adjust Mail Settings

1. Open the Mail application and choose Mail⇨Preferences.

2. On the General tab, choose how often you want Mail to check for new messages. In Figure 8-17, Mail was configured to check for mail every 15 minutes.

3. Click the Accounts button, click Mailbox Behaviors and choose how long you want to wait before deleted messages are emptied from the Trash. The default interval is one week.

4. Click the Junk Mail button and adjust junk mail filtering settings.

    When you first start using Mail, you should leave the junk mail filter in Training mode. If you set it to Automatic mode, Mail may inadvertently junk otherwise valid e-mail.

5. Click Fonts & Colors and choose default fonts and colors for e-mail composition and viewing.

6. Click the Composing button. If you participate in e-mail lists that require plain text, choose Plain Text in the Message Format menu, as shown in Figure 8-18.

    If you want to reply to rich text messages in rich text format, select Use the Same Message Format as the Original Message.

7. Close the Preferences window after you're done making settings adjustments.

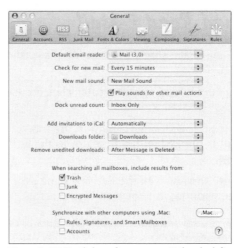

Figure 8-17: Decide how often you want Mail to check for new messages.

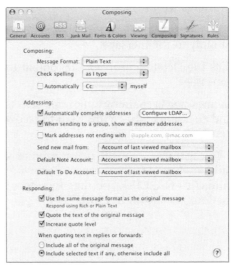

Figure 8-18: Mail can be configured for plain text mail.

Create a To Do Item from an E-Mail

1. Open Apple Mail and click To Do on the toolbar.

    If the To Do list doesn't open automatically, click your e-mail account under To Do in the sidebar on the left side of the Mail application window.

2. Click in the Title field and enter a descriptive title, as shown in Figure 8-19.

3. Enter a date in the Date Due field.

    If you have a two-button mouse, right-click the Date Due field and choose a day. Otherwise, simply enter a calendar date in the Date Due field. You can also choose Reveal in iCal to display To Do items in iCal.

4. Click Priority and select a priority level for the item from the menu that appears.

5. To set up an alarm for the item, click the Alarm icon and set a date and time for a reminder alarm. In Figure 8-19, two alarms have been set.

6. When an Alarm message appears, as shown in Figure 8-20, note the reminder and then click the Close button to dismiss the Alarm.

7. After you complete the To Do item, place a check mark next to it in the Apple Mail To Do list.

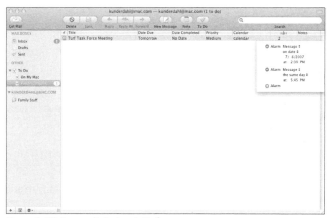

Figure 8-19: Set up a To Do item in Mail.

Figure 8-20: Set up an alarm.

Subscribe to an RSS Feed

1. Look for an RSS (Really Simple Syndication) icon on a Web site that you regularly visit.

    Many Web sites, including www.dummies.com, have a Sign Up for RSS Feeds link. Click this link to sign up for feeds.

2. Click the RSS icon to review the feed, as shown in Figure 8-21.

3. To sign up for the feed, click Subscribe in Mail under Actions on the right side of the screen.

4. To view updates, launch Mail and click the name of the feed in the Sidebar, as shown in Figure 8-22.

5. To unsubscribe from a feed, click the feed in the Mail Sidebar to select it. Click the Actions button at the bottom of the sidebar (the button has a toothed gear icon on it) and choose Delete from the menu that appears. Click Delete to confirm the deletion.

    You can also subscribe to RSS feeds directly from within Apple Mail. Launch Mail and choose File➪Add RSS Feeds and then browse to a feed that interests you.

    The steps shown here assume that you're using Safari as your Web browser.

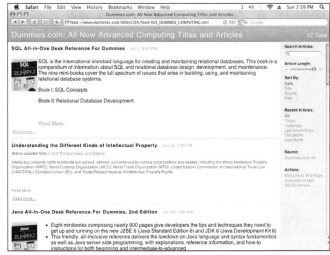

Figure 8-21: Dummies.com is one of many web sites offering RSS feeds.

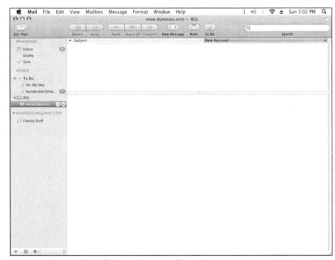

Figure 8-22: Read RSS feed updates in Mail.

Using a .Mac Account

One of the coolest things about the Internet is that anyone can publish photos, blogs, and other stuff for the whole world to see. If you'd like your own online home page, you're going to need some online real estate on which to build it. Many different companies offer online server space, but such servers are often costly or difficult to use.

Apple offers online server space, too, and it's much easier to use than many other online services. The Apple online service is .Mac, and you can use .Mac for both public and private purposes. On the public side, you can use .Mac to publish photos, videos, calendars, and Web pages, and on the private side, you can use .Mac to archive important files and data so that it can be easily retrieved from anywhere in the world. .Mac also helps you create your own blogs and podcasts, set up personalized e-mail accounts, and more.

A .Mac account costs about $100 per year. This is close to what other online server space companies charge, but with .Mac you get user friendliness for no extra charge. You can also try .Mac for free for 60 days. This chapter shows you how to get started with a .Mac account and how to start using some of the most popular .Mac features.

Chapter

9

Get ready to . . .

Create a .Mac Account

1. Visit Apple's .Mac Web site at `www.apple.com/dotmac`.

2. Click the link to either sign up for a free trial or sign up immediately for an account.

3. Follow the onscreen instructions to create your account, as shown in Figure 9-1. Choose your Member Name carefully because you can't change it later.

 If the Member Name you choose is already taken, the .Mac Web site will prompt you to enter a different user name.

4. Print your account information when prompted to do so. This information — including server addresses — is important and is needed later.

 The e-mail address, e-mail server address, and Simple Mail Transport Protocol (SMTP) server address can be used to set up almost any e-mail program to use your .Mac account.

5. Log in to .Mac when you're prompted to do so, as shown in Figure 9-2.

6. After you're done using .Mac, click the Log Out link in the upper-right corner of the screen.

7. To log in to your .Mac account from any Internet-connected computer, simply visit `www.apple.com`, click the .Mac link, and then click the Log In link in the upper-right corner.

 If you access .Mac from a computer other than your own (especially a public computer), don't allow the browser to remember your password and make sure that you log out when you're done.

Figure 9-1: Choose your Member Name carefully.

Figure 9-2: Log in to your new .Mac account.

Backup Files

1. Visit www.apple.com/dotmac and click the .Mac Log In link to log in to your .Mac account.

2. Click the iDisk link and then enter your .Mac username and password again to log in to iDisk.

    Don't append @mac.com to your username when logging in to iDisk.

3. In the list of iDisk folders that appears, as shown in Figure 9-3, double-click the folder to which you want to upload files.

    To create a subfolder, click New Folder and then type a name for the new folder. When the new folder is created, double-click it to open it.

4. When you're in the proper folder, click Upload.

5. In the Select a File to Upload dialog box, click Choose a File.

6. Use the Finder to locate a file you want to upload, as shown in Figure 9-4. Click a file to select it and then click Choose.

7. In the Select a File to Upload dialog box, click Upload. After the file is done uploading, it appears in the list of files on iDisk.

    To delete a file from iDisk, select the file on iDisk and then click the Delete link in the far-right column. The Delete link is a circle with a slash. To download a file, click the Download link, which is the down-pointing arrow in the far-right column. Downloaded files remain on iDisk until you delete them.

Figure 9-3: Double-click the folder to which you want to upload files.

Figure 9-4: Browse to the file that you want to upload.

Publish Photos Online

1. Log in to .Mac and then open iDisk, as described in the preceding section.

2. Double-click the Pictures folder to open it.

3. In the Pictures folder, click Upload.

 If you want to share only certain files in your iDisk Pictures folder, create a subfolder, as described in the preceding section, and upload the pictures you want to share to that subfolder.

4. In the Select a File to Upload dialog box, click Choose a File.

5. Use the Finder to locate a picture you want to share, as shown in Figure 9-5. Click a file to select it and then click Choose.

6. In the Select a File to Upload dialog box, click Upload. After the file is done uploading, it appears in the list of files on iDisk.

7. Repeat Steps 3–6 until all the pictures you want to share are uploaded.

8. Close iDisk after you're done uploading files.

9. In your .Mac account, click the My Pages link and then click the Photo Album tab.

10. Browse through the available photo album themes, as shown in Figure 9-6.

11. Click a theme to select it.

Figure 9-5: Select pictures to share.

Figure 9-6: Choose a theme for your online photo album.

12. Select the folder containing the pictures you want to share, as shown in Figure 9-7. If the pictures are in a subfolder, make sure you select that subfolder.

13. Click Choose when the proper folder is selected.

14. Enter an album name and description in the screen that appears.

15. Type a description or caption under each picture, if desired.

 If you don't want a particular photo to appear in the album, deselect Show on that picture's thumbnail.

16. Scroll to the bottom of the album screen. If you want a view counter to appear in the album, select Show by the counter. You can also choose to show a Send Me a Message link, if you want.

17. Click Preview near the top of the screen to preview the photo album as it will appear to visitors. If you want to make further changes, click Edit.

18. When you're ready to publish the album, click Publish near the top of the screen. A Web page appears displaying the Web address for your photo album.

19. Click the Web address to open the photo album, as shown in Figure 9-8.

20. Copy the Web address and send it to friends, family, and anyone else with whom you want to share the album.

 Click a picture's thumbnail to view the full-quality image. Click Start Slideshow to view a slideshow of your images in a new browser window.

Figure 9-7: Select the folder containing pictures for your online photo album.

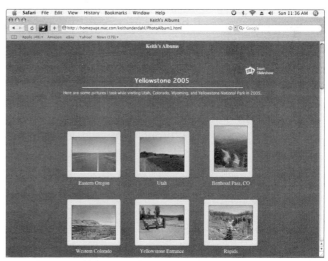

Figure 9-8: Your published photo album can be viewed by anyone on the Internet.

Synchronize Computers through a .Mac Account

1. Open System Preferences and then click the .Mac icon to open .Mac preferences.

2. Enter your .Mac member name and password on the Sign In screen, as shown in Figure 9-9.

 Do not append @mac.com to your .Mac Member Name.

3. Click Sync to open the Synchronization options.

4. Place a check mark next to Synchronize with .Mac, as shown in Figure 9-10.

5. Choose whether you want synchronization to happen automatically, manually, or at specific intervals. In Figure 9-10, synchronizations happen automatically.

6. Place a check mark next to the items you want to synchronize.

7. If you chose Manual or Specific Interval synchronization, click Sync Now.

8. Repeat the above steps on other computers that you wish to synchronize through .Mac.

 If you receive an error message on other computers that they're not registered to synchronize through .Mac, click Advanced in the .Mac System Preferences window and then click Register this Computer.

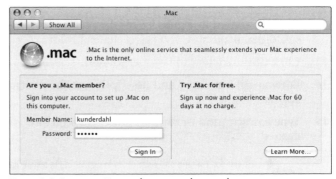

Figure 9-9: Enter your .Mac member name and password.

Figure 9-10: Choose how and what you want to synchronize.

Read and Send .Mac E-Mail

1. Log in to .Mac and then click the Mail link.

> You can log in to .Mac and check your .Mac e-mail by using almost any Web browser on any computer connected to the Internet. The Apple Mail program (and some other e-mail clients) can also be used to access a .Mac e-mail account. See Chapter 8 for more on using Apple Mail.

2. To download e-mail, click the Get Mail button near the top of the .Mac Inbox, as shown in Figure 9-11.

3. To read a message, click it in the Inbox to open the message, as shown in Figure 9-12.

4. Use the controls at the top of the screen to Delete, Reply, or Forward the message.

5. To return to the Inbox, click Mail in the upper-left corner.

6. Click Compose to compose a new e-mail message.

7. After you're done composing your e-mail, click Send.

> Click Attach to attach a file to the e-mail. When the attachment window appears, click Choose File and browse to the file that you want to attach. Select the file, click Choose, and then click Attach in the Attachment window. Click Apply after you're done attaching files. Remember, some people are limited on the size of file attachments they can receive in e-mail, so avoid e-mailing large files.

Figure 9-11: Use .Mac to check e-mail with any Internet-connected computer.

Figure 9-12: Reading and sending .Mac e-mail is easy!

Blogging and Web Designing with iWeb

*N*ot so long ago, keeping in touch with distant friends and family meant writing letters, stuffing envelopes, and licking stamps. And if you wanted to share some favorite photos, you had to get expensive film duplicates made by a photo processor.

The Internet has revolutionized the way we keep in touch. E-mail is one great way to communicate with distant relations, and you can also create your own Web site. When you create a Web page and put it online, anyone with Internet access can read your story and see your pictures. And you don't have to be a trained Web developer to produce your own online presence because Apple produces a good Web design program called *iWeb*. iWeb is bundled with many new Macs, or you can purchase it as part of the iLife suite from your favorite Apple retailer.

This chapter shows you how to create a Web page with iWeb and how to upload your Web page to the Internet so that anyone can see it. Steps also show you how to create and share

- **Blogs:** Short for *Weblogs*, blogs are daily or weekly narratives that you post online for others to read. Blogs may focus on your travels, politics, hobbies, your life in general, or any other subject that you can imagine.

- **Podcasts:** — A Podcast is like a mix between a blog and a radio or TV show. You can record your own Podcasts, which can then be shared with others through iTunes.

Your Web pages must be uploaded to a Web server before others can view them. This chapter assumes that you use .Mac as your Web server. For more on creating and using a .Mac account, see Chapter 9.

Create a Web Page

1. Launch iWeb from the Dock or from the Applications folder.

   The first time you launch iWeb, you may be asked to confirm keychain access for your .Mac account. Choose Allow Once to log in to .Mac only this time, or choose Always Allow if you always want iWeb to connect to your .Mac account.

2. In the Template window that appears, as shown in Figure 10-1, select a theme for your Web site in the list of themes on the left.

3. After you choose a theme, choose a page style from the list of pages on the right.

4. Click Choose.

5. In the page that's created, click in a text area to replace placeholder text with your own, as shown in Figure 10-2.

6. To change text formatting, click and drag over the text you want to change and click Inspector in the iWeb toolbar.

7. When the Inspector window appears in the upper-right corner of the screen, as shown in Figure 10-2, click the T button to open the Text Inspector.

8. Use the menus and options in the Text Inspector to change text formatting. If you want to create a numbered or bulleted list, as shown in Figure 10-2, click the List button in the Text Inspector and then choose a list style in the Bullets & Numbering menu.

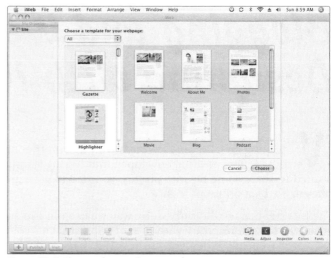

Figure 10-1: Choose a theme and page template.

Figure 10-2: Replace the placeholder text with your own.

9. To replace a placeholder picture with a photo of your own, open a Finder window and browse to a picture that you want to use on your Web page.

10. Arrange the Finder and iWeb windows so that they're both visible, as shown in Figure 10-3, and then click and drag the photo from the Finder to iWeb.

11. To add a new page to your Web site, choose File⇨New Page and then choose a page template for the new page, as shown in Figure 10-1.

12. To change the name of a page, double-click it in the list of pages on the left side of the screen and then type a new name.

 Don't use spaces in file names. For best results, try to use descriptive single-word names for all your Web pages.

13. To create a hyperlink, click and drag to select some text on which you want to create a link.

14. Open the Inspector if it isn't already open and then click the Link Inspector button (a blue circle with an arrow).

15. Select Enable as a Hyperlink.

16. In the Link To menu, choose whether you want to link to one of your own pages, an external page, a file, or an e-mail message.

17. Choose a specific target for the link in the second menu or field. If you're linking to one of your own pages, choose the page, as shown in Figure 10-4.

 Don't forget to save your work periodically. Choose File⇨Save to save your changes.

Figure 10-3: Click and drag photos into iWeb.

Figure 10-4: Use the Link Inspector to create hyperlinks.

Upload the Web Page to a Web Server

1. After you're done creating your Web site, choose File➪Save to save your work.

2. Choose File➪Publish All to .Mac, as shown in Figure 10-5.

3. Read the warning message that appears about copyrighted content and then click Continue when you're sure that your Web site is in compliance with copyright laws.

4. If iWeb tells you that Publish will work in the background, click OK. Your Web site takes longer to publish if it includes many pictures.

5. When the site is completely uploaded, make a note of the Web address listed in the notification tab that appears. This is the address that others will use to visit your Web site.

6. Click Visit Site Now in the notification tab.

7. Test your Web site in your Web browser, as shown in Figure 10-6. Make sure that links function and that images display properly.

 If possible, test your Web site in several different browser applications, such as Safari and Firefox. If possible, also test the site with Internet Explorer on a Windows PC.

 If you use a Web server other than .Mac, in iWeb choose File➪ Publish to a Folder and then choose a folder on your hard drive in which the Web site should be stored. Use a File Transfer Protocol (FTP) program to upload your Web site to the server following the instructions provided by the Web server's administrator.

Figure 10-5: Publish your site to .Mac.

Figure 10-6: Test the Web site in multiple browser applications.

Create a Weblog

1. Launch iWeb and create a Web site, as described earlier in this chapter.

2. Choose File⊅New Page.

3. Choose the theme for your Web site on the left and then locate the Blog template on the right.

4. Click the Blog template and then click Choose.

5. Enter your own personalized text and pictures, as described earlier in this chapter.

6. To add a Weblog entry, click Entries in the Site Organizer on the left side of the screen and then click Add Entry in the list of blog entries at the top of the screen, as shown in Figure 10-7.

 All blog entries appear in the list. To delete an entry, select it in the list and click Delete Entry.

7. When a new blog screen appears in the lower part of the iWeb window, type the day's entry.

8. Click the main blog entry in the Site Organizer and update your personal information, as shown in Figure 10-8.

 After your initial update of the Weblog's front page, the page updates automatically every time you make a new entry.

Figure 10-7: Click Add Entry to create a new blog entry.

Figure 10-8: Personalize the front page for your blog.

Publish Your Weblog Online

1. After you're done editing your Weblog in iWeb, choose File➪Publish All to .Mac, as shown in Figure 10-9.

2. Confirm that you have the right to publish the contents of your Weblog and follow the instructions onscreen to upload all files.

    Remember, you must re-upload your Weblog every time you add an entry. Make sure that you choose Publish All to .Mac in the File menu to ensure that all blog-related files are uploaded.

3. After the files are uploaded, choose File➪Visit Published Site to test the site in a Web browser.

4. Click the Blog link to view the Weblog.

5. To subscribe to the RSS feed, click the RSS Subscribe link on the blog page and then read the RSS entries, as shown in Figure 10-10.

    RSS feeds send automatic notices to readers when your Weblog changes. Readers who want to subscribe to your Weblog must have an RSS-capable Web browser or other program that can use RSS feeds. Safari is RSS-capable, but Mozilla Firefox is not.

    RSS feeds can be added to OS X Leopard Dashboard. See Chapter 7 for more on adding RSS feeds to Dashboard.

Figure 10-9: Choose File➪Publish All to .Mac to upload your complete Weblog.

Figure 10-10: Users with RSS-capable browsers can subscribe to your Weblog.

Record a Podcast

1. Launch GarageBand (like iWeb, GarageBand is part of the iLife suite) from the Dock or the Applications folder.

2. Click New Podcast Episode in the GarageBand splash screen that appears.

3. In the New Project window, type a file name for the Podcast and click Create.

4. In the list of audio tracks, click the Male Voice or Female Voice (as appropriate) track and make sure that a microphone is connected to your Mac.

5. Click the Record button and start recording your Podcast. Click Stop when you're done.

 Try to record in as quiet an area as possible. Even things like noisy computer fans or air blowing through heat ducts can foul the quality of your audio recording. Also, consider hanging blankets or drapes on the walls to minimize sound reflection.

6. Choose Share⇨Send Podcast to iWeb, as shown in Figure 10-11.

7. When the Podcast appears on a new blog page in iWeb, as shown in Figure 10-12, edit the text of the page. The text should describe the subject of the Podcast.

8. In iWeb, choose File⇨Publish All to .Mac to upload your Podcast and other changes.

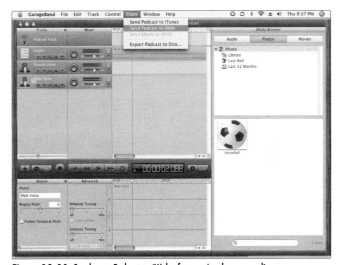

Figure 10-11: Send your Podcast to iWeb after you're done recording.

Figure 10-12: Edit the text on the Podcast page.

Chatting on Your Mac

Although the Internet has only been in widespread use for a little over a decade, its roots go all the way back to the late 1960s. One of the earliest uses for the Internet was *live chat* — distant parties typed messages to each other in real time. This chat tradition continues today and is made easy by instant messaging programs, such as AOL Instant Messenger (AIM), MSN Messenger, ICQ, and Apple's iChat. Not only does iChat give you access to the .Mac network of chat users, but it can be configured to work with some other popular instant messaging networks as well.

In addition to typed text messages, some chat programs now offer voice chat as well. Real time voice chat may not seem revolutionary to anyone who has ever used a telephone, but the free or nearly-free cost of Internet-based voice chat appeals to anyone who has ever paid a long distance phone bill. iChat can be configured to work with popular voice networks, including Skype and Google Talk.

This chapter shows you how to chat via iChat. It also shows you how to configure iChat for use with the Skype and Google Talk voice networks. Finally, this chapter also shows you how to use a third-party chat program — Adium — which is available for Mac. Adium can be used with many of the most popular instant messaging networks, including AOL Instant Messenger, MSN, ICQ, Yahoo, and more.

Chapter 11

Get ready to . . .

Set Up iChat

1. Launch iChat from the Dock or the Applications folder.

2. If this is the first time you're launching iChat, enter your .Mac or AIM account information, as shown in Figure 11-1, and then click Continue.

3. Click Done when you're done setting up your iChat account.

4. If you use a Jabber chat account, choose iChat⇨ Preferences, click the Accounts button, and then click the Add Account button (it looks like a plus sign) in the lower-left corner of the Preferences window. Choose Jabber in the Account Type menu and enter your Jabber account information.

Google Talk — which is covered in the next task — is a Jabber account.

5. If you want to be able to easily chat with other people on your local network, open iChat Preferences, click the Accounts button, and place a check mark next to Use Bonjour Messaging.

If you enable Bonjour, you may see a warning message about your Firewall settings. If you see this warning, click the Open Sharing Prefs button. In Sharing preferences, click Firewall and then place a check mark next to iChat Bonjour. Close Sharing preferences when you're done. See Chapter 20 for more on working with the Mac OS X Firewall.

6. To add a chat partner, choose Buddies⇨Add Buddy and then click New Person.

7. Enter an account name or an e-mail address in the window, as shown in Figure 11-2, and then click Add.

Figure 11-1: Enter your chat account information here.

If you don't yet have a .Mac or other iChat-compatible account, click the Get an iChat Account button and follow the instructions onscreen to create an account. For more on getting and using a .Mac account, see Chapter 9.

Figure 11-2: Add chat buddies to your Address Book.

Chat using iChat

1. To chat with someone, double-click the person's name in your list of chat buddies.

2. Type a message, as shown in Figure 11-3, and then press Return to send the message.

    If you receive a chat message from a buddy, click in the chat window that appears automatically to begin chatting.

3. To add a smiley to your chat message, click the smiley icon on the right side of the text box and choose a smiley from the menu that appears.

4. If you're leaving the computer for a while, choose iChat➪My Status and then choose a status (such as Out to Lunch or On the Phone) from the menu that appears.

5. To change your account picture, choose iChat➪Change My Picture. In the Buddy Picture window, as shown in Figure 11-4, click Choose and browse to a new picture. Click Open to select the picture and then click Set to close the Buddy Picture window and set your new picture.

6. To change the font or chat balloon colors used when you chat, choose iChat➪Preferences and then click Messages. Use the color menus to change the color of your balloons or text and click Set Font to choose a different font and size.

    If incoming text is too small or too hard to read, place a check mark next to Reformat Incoming Messages and then click Set Font to choose a bigger, easier-to-read font.

Figure 11-3: Type messages and press Return to send them.

 You can add additional chat accounts at any time. Choose iChat➪ Preferences, click the Accounts button, and then click the Add button (it looks like a plus sign) in the lower-left corner of the Accounts screen. Enter the account name and password for the account in the window that appears.

Figure 11-4: Select a new Buddy image here.

Sharing Your Screen with iChat

1. Launch iChat from the Dock or Applications folder.

2. Begin a chat with a buddy, as I describe earlier in this chapter.

3. To access your chat partner's screen, choose Buddies⇨ Share . . . and choose the buddy's name.

4. If you receive a request to share your screen, as shown in Figure 11-5, click Accept to accept the request or Decline if you don't want to allow sharing.

    Click Text Reply if you wish to ask the buddy a question or send a message before you start screen sharing.

5. To control screen sharing, use the window, as shown in Figure 11-6, to perform the following tasks:

   • **Stop:** Click the X (Stop) button to stop screen sharing.

   • **Screen:** Click the Screen button (it looks like a cube) to view your buddy's screen.

   • **Audio:** Click the Audio button (it looks like a micro-phone) to toggle audio on and off. You can also adjust volume using the volume slider under the Audio button.

    To immediately stop screen sharing at any time, press Control+Esc.

Figure 11-5: Click Accept to share your screen.

Figure 11-6: Use this window to control screen sharing.

Use Google Talk with iChat

1. Launch iChat from the Dock or Applications folder.

2. Choose iChat➪Preferences to open the Preferences dialog.

3. Click Accounts at the top of the Preferences dialog and then click the Add button (it looks like a plus sign) in the lower-left corner of the Accounts window.

4. In the Account Type menu, choose Jabber Account, as shown in Figure 11-7.

5. Enter your Gmail e-mail address in the Account Name, as shown in Figure 11-7.

 A Gmail e-mail account is required to use Google Talk.

6. Enter your Gmail password in the Password field and enter gmail.com in the Server field.

7. Click Add to create the account and then close the Accounts preferences window.

8. In iChat, choose Window➪Show Jabber List to view your list of Google Talk buddies, as shown in Figure 11-8.

9. To start an audio chat with a Google Talk buddy, click the name of the buddy in your Jabber List and then click the Audio Chat button (it looks like a telephone) at the bottom of the Jabber List window.

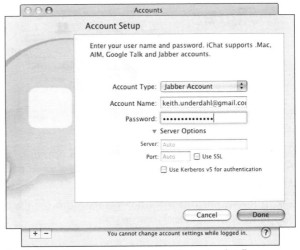

Figure 11-7: Create a new Jabber account with your Google Talk account.

Figure 11-8: Use the Jabber window to chat with your Google Talk buddies.

Install Skype

1. Visit www.skype.com and follow the instructions on the Skype Web site to download Skype for Mac.

2. After Skype is done downloading, double-click the downloaded disk image (.dmg) file to mount the installer's disk image. Click Continue if you see an application warning.

3. In the Finder window that appears, click and drag the Skype icon to the Applications folder, as shown in Figure 11-9.

4. Open the Applications folder and then double-click the Skype icon to launch the program.

 If you want to add Skype to the Dock, open the Applications folder and then click and drag the Skype icon to the Dock.

5. Read and accept the Skype license agreement.

6. If you already have a Skype account, enter your Skype name and password, as shown in Figure 11-10.If you don't have an account, click Don't Have a Skype Name and create an account using the dialog that appears.

 If you do not yet have a Skype account, click the Don't Have a Skype Name link and then enter a name and password to create a new account in the window that appears. Click Create to create the account. If the name you entered is already taken, a warning message advises you of this fact.

7. Click Sign In to sign in to Skype.

 The first time you log in to Skype you may be prompted to update your account's personal information. Update the information as desired and click Apply to close the account profile window.

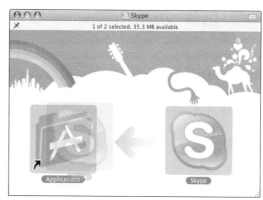

Figure 11-9: Click and drag Skype to the Applications folder.

Figure 11-10: Enter your Skype name and password.

Place Calls Using Skype

1. Launch Skype from the Applications folder.

2. Type a Skype name or phone number in the text field at the top of the Skype window.

3. If the name isn't in your Contact list, click Search for Skype Name when the link appears, as shown in Figure 11-11.

4. In the Skype search window that appears, wait for the search results to finish. When you see the listing for the person you want to call, click the name to select it and then click Add Contact.

5. Click the name of a person you want to call and then click the Call button (it's green and looks like a telephone).

6. When the Call window appears, as shown in Figure 11-12, you're connected. Begin speaking.

7. To disconnect from a call, click the red Hang Up button in the lower-right corner of the Call window.

 You can also do text chats with Skype. Click the user's name and then click the Text Chat button (it's blue and looks like a cartoon speech balloon) next to the name. Text chat is a useful feature if a poor Internet connection or hardware troubles prevent one party from hearing or speaking.

 To set up a conference call with multiple parties, choose Call⇨Start Conference Call. Select members for the call in the Start Conference window that appears and then click Start. Conference calls work best if everyone on the call has a fast Internet connection.

Figure 11-11: Use the Skype search function to find contacts.

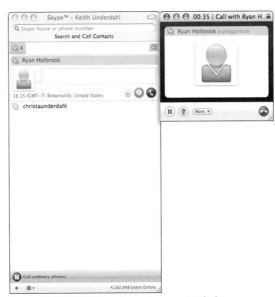

Figure 11-12: Make free calls over the Internet with Skype.

Text Chat with Adium

1. Visit www.adiumx.com and follow the instructions on the Web site to download Adium.

2. After the download is complete, locate and double-click the disk image (.dmg) file for the installer and then drag the Adium icon to the Applications folder shortcut that appears in the Adium window.

3. Open your Applications folder and double-click the Adium icon to launch the program.

4. In the Preferences: Accounts window that appears the first time you launch Adium, click the Add Account button (it looks like a plus sign in the lower-left corner) and choose an account type, as shown in Figure 11-13.

5. Enter the account name and password for your chat account in the window that appears and then click OK to create the account.

6. Close the Preferences: Accounts window after you're done adding accounts and making other changes.

To re-open the Preferences window later and add more accounts, choose Adium⇨Preferences.

7. Double-click a contact in your list of contacts and begin typing a message, as shown in Figure 11-14.

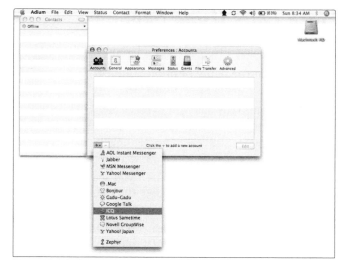

Figure 11-13: Choose an account type to configure in Adium.

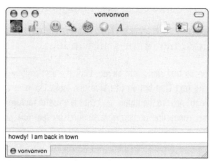

Figure 11-14: Adium can be used with most popular chat networks.

Part 4
Using Multimedia

The 5th Wave   By Rich Tennant

Using iTunes and iPods

More than almost any other company, Apple has become associated with digital music in the last few years. The iPod has become the world's most popular and identifiable MP3 player, and the iTunes program revolutionized online music sales at a time when downloadable songs looked like they might be litigated out of existence.

iPods and iTunes get along just fine with Windows PCs, but because you have a Macintosh, the integration couldn't be more simple. No matter what iPod you have — ranging from a tiny iPod Nano to a full size (yet still compact) iPod — it is recognized instantly when you connect the iPod to your Mac. And because iTunes is the program for synchronizing music to an iPod, it goes without saying that your Mac already has the necessary software to copy songs and videos to your iPod. This chapter shows you how to quickly and easily use an iPod with your Mac.

Of course, you don't need an iPod to use iTunes. Even if you have no MP3 player at all, iTunes is a great program for storing, organizing, and playing songs, videos, audio books, and other multimedia files. This chapter shows you how to manage and play your multimedia library with iTunes.

 To ensure you have the latest version of iTunes, run Software Update, as described in Chapter 4, or visit www.apple.com/itunes.

Chapter 12

Get ready to . . .

Import Music from CDs

1. Insert a music CD into the disc drive on your computer.

2. When iTunes opens, wait several seconds for iTunes to obtain data — the data may include song titles, artist names, and album titles — about the music CD.

    If iTunes doesn't obtain song data automatically, choose Advanced⇨Get CD Track Names. Your computer must be connected to the Internet to obtain song data.

3. Remove the check mark next to the songs you don't want to import. In Figure 12-1, the last song on the CD was deselected.

4. If you wish to manually modify a data field (such as the song name or genre), click the field once to select it, wait about two seconds, and then click it again. Type a new entry.

5. Click Import CD to import songs. In Figure 12-2, the first song has been completely imported, and the second song is in the process of being imported.

6. After all the songs are imported, click the Eject Disc button in the lower-right corner of the iTunes window.

    When you start to import music, iTunes begins playing the imported songs. The import occurs slightly faster if you stop playback.

Figure 12-1: Select which songs you want to import.

Figure 12-2: Songs import faster if you stop playback.

Create a Playlist

1. Launch iTunes.

2. Choose File⇨Create Smart Playlist.

   You can also quickly create a new empty playlist by choosing File⇨New Playlist.

3. In the Smart Playlist dialog box that appears, choose a category — such as Artist, Genre, or Comment — in the first menu.

4. Choose a condition — such as Contains or Does Not Contain — in the second menu.

5. Type a criterion in the third menu.

6. To add additional criteria, as shown in Figure 12-3, click the plus sign to the right of the third menu. In Figure 12-3, a playlist is created by using songs in the Jazz and Blues genres.

   When using multiple rules, choose Any or All in the Match menu at the top of the Smart Playlist dialog box, as appropriate.

7. Choose other criteria for the playlist and then click OK.

8. After the playlist is created, type a descriptive name for the playlist in the Source pane on the left side of the screen, as shown in Figure 12-4.

9. To add songs to a smart playlist, choose File⇨Edit Smart Playlist and repeat the above steps to add more songs.

   For regular playlists, simply click and drag songs from the Library to the playlist in the Source pane.

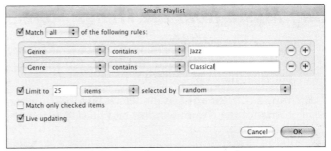

Figure 12-3: Smart playlists offer a faster way to create playlists.

Figure 12-4: Give your playlist a descriptive name.

Buy Music from the iTunes Store

1. Launch iTunes, make sure your computer is connected to the Internet, and then click iTunes Store in the Source pane, as shown in Figure 12-5.

2. Type a song or artist in the search box in the upper-right corner of the iTunes window and press Return to begin your search.

3. Review the search results. To hear a preview, double-click a song. A 30-second preview of the song downloads and plays.

4. When you find a song that you want to buy, click Buy Song in the far-right column of the song list.

5. If you already have an Apple or AOL account, enter your ID and password in the login screen, as shown in Figure 12-6.

 If you do not yet have an account, click Create New Account and follow the instructions onscreen to create an account. You need a credit card to create your account. After you're done creating the account and logged in, you need to re-click the Buy Song link.

6. When you see the confirmation window, review the song or album you're about to buy and then click Buy. The status area at the top of the iTunes screen shows the progress of the purchase and download.

 You can disable the confirmation message by placing a check mark next to Don't Ask Me about Buying Songs Again, but it is not recommended.

Figure 12-5: Click Music Store to open the iTunes store.

Figure 12-6: Log in to the iTunes store with your Apple or AOL account.

Listen to Internet Radio

1. Launch iTunes and click Radio in the Source pane on the left side of the screen.

2. Click an arrow next to a category to expand the listing, as shown in Figure 12-7.

3. Double-click a radio station to begin playing it.

    If the radio station broadcast frequently cuts out while the signal is buffered, choose a different station with a lower bit rate. For example, if you have a dial-up Internet connection, you probably can't listen to radio stations with a bit rate greater than 48 kbps.

4. When you find a favorite radio station that you'll want to hear again later, click and drag the station to the Radio Stations playlist in the Source Pane, as shown in Figure 12-8.

    Radio stations can be added to any playlist. If you don't see a Radio Stations playlist in your iTunes window, you can create one or create new radio station playlists.

    Most playback features — such as Next Track and Pause — don't work while listening to streaming Internet radio. Like broadcast radio, you can only turn Internet radio on or off or adjust the volume.

Figure 12-7: Browse for an Internet radio station.

Figure 12-8: Save your favorite radio stations in playlists.

Export Songs to an iPod

1. Connect the iPod to your Mac.

    You can connect the iPod directly to your Mac's Universal Serial Bus (USB) port. Alternatively, you may use an iPod Dock or USB extension cable.

2. If iTunes doesn't launch automatically, launch iTunes from the Dock or the Applications folder.

3. Select songs that you want to add to the iPod.

    To select multiple songs, hold down the ⌘ key while clicking each song you want to add. To select a series of songs, select the first song and then hold down the Shift key while clicking the last song. All songs between the first and last song are selected.

4. Click and drag songs to the iPod in the Source pane, as shown in Figure 12-9.

5. To automatically fill space on the iPod, click the iPod in the Source pane to open its contents.

6. In the Autofill From menu near the bottom of the iTunes window, select a folder or playlist from which you want Autofill to select songs.

7. Remove the check mark next to Replace All Songs When Autofilling, as shown in Figure 12-10.

8. Click Autofill. The iPod is filled automatically with songs from your iTunes library.

Figure 12-9: Select songs that you want to add to the iPod.

Figure 12-10: Autofill quickly copies songs from your library to your iPod.

Adjust iPod Settings

1. Launch iTunes and connect the iPod to your computer.

2. Click the iPod in the source pane, and then click the Settings tab in the main iTunes window.

3. Scroll down the Settings window to the Options section, as shown in Figure 12-11.

4. If you're concerned about storage space, place a check mark next to Convert Higher Bit Rate Songs to 128 kbps AAC for This iPod.

5. Review other options and click Apply to save your changes to the iPod.

Delete Media from an iPod

1. Connect the iPod to your computer and launch iTunes.

2. Click the iPod in the Source pane to display its contents.

3. Select a song or songs that you want to delete from the iPod.

 To select multiple songs, hold down the ⌘ key while clicking each song.

4. Press the Delete key or choose Edit⇨Delete, as shown in Figure 12-12.

Figure 12-11: Adjust settings for your iPod here.

Figure 12-12: Removing songs takes only seconds.

Store Data Files on Your iPod

1. Open iPod settings, as described earlier in this chapter, and place a check mark next to Enable Disk Use.

2. Adjust the Disk Use slider to determine how much space will be reserved for songs and data and then click OK to close the Settings window.

3. Use the Finder to click and drag files to the iPod, as shown in Figure 12-13.

4. Click and drag the iPod's Desktop icon to the Trash to manually eject the iPod.

Play Music on Your Stereo with AirTunes

1. Install and configure an AirTunes-compatible AirPort Base Station, as described in Chapter 17. The Base Station's documentation will note whether it supports AirTunes. Connect powered audio speakers or another audio device to the audio output on the AirPort Base Station.

2. Open the Applications folder on your Mac, open the Utilities subfolder, and then double-click the AirPort Utility icon.

3. Click the Base Station name, as shown in Figure 12-14, click Continue, and then choose Manual Setup in the message that appears.

4. Enter the password for the Base Station and then click OK to log in to the Base Station.

Figure 12-13: You can use an iPod to quickly transfer data files.

When the iPod's status light glows solid green, it can be safely disconnected from the computer's USB port.

Figure 12-14: Select the AirTunes-compatible Base Station and click Configure.

5. In the Base Station Configuration Utility, click Music to open AirTunes options.

6. Place a check mark next to Enable AirTunes, as shown in Figure 12-15.

7. Provide a descriptive name for the speakers that are connected to the Base Station in the iTunes Speaker Name field.

8. Click Update to upload your changes to the Base Station.

9. After the Base Station has restarted (its status light glows solid green), launch iTunes and find a playlist or songs that you want to play.

10. Choose the appropriate speakers from the Speakers menu at the bottom of the iTunes window, as shown in Figure 12-16.

 To play music to multiple speaker locations, choose Multiple Speakers and then place a check mark next to each set of speakers listed in the resulting window.

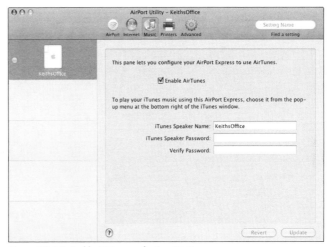

Figure 12-15: Enable AirTunes on the Base Station.

Figure 12-16: Select the AirTunes speakers.

Working with Third Party MP3 Players

When it comes to MP3 players, Macs and iPods seem to go hand-in-hand. But lots of MP3 players are made by companies other than Apple, and if you're reading this chapter, you probably have one of these third-party players.

Because you have one of these players, you may be wondering if it's compatible with your Mac, especially if the player's instructions only tell you how to use it with a Windows PC. Fortunately, most MP3 players can be used with a Mac, although you probably can't use iTunes for copying media files and playlists directly to the player. Instead, you'll have to use the Finder. This chapter shows you how to

➡ Connect a third-party MP3 player to your Mac.

➡ Copy music files to the MP3 player.

➡ Create folders on the MP3 player in which to organize media.

➡ Delete music from the MP3 player.

 The steps in this chapter apply to most third-party MP3 players, but it's possible that your particular player is uniquely incompatible with your Mac. Some players require proprietary software in order to access directories and copy files to the player. If you can't seem to follow the steps in this chapter with your MP3 player, check the manufacturer's Web site for special instructions or information regarding Mac compatibility. A few third-party players actually support iTunes. If you connect the player to your computer and it appears in the Devices list in iTunes, you should be able to use iTunes (see Chapter 12) to manage media on the player.

Get ready to . . .

Connect the MP3 Player to Your Mac

1. Connect the MP3 player to your Mac's Universal Serial Bus (USB) port.

2. Look for the player's icon to appear on your Desktop as an Untitled disk volume, as shown in Figure 13-1.

    If the MP3 player doesn't appear, make sure the unit's power is turned on.

3. Before disconnecting the MP3 player from your USB port, drag its icon to the Trash icon on the Dock to unmount the volume. When the MP3 player's icon no longer appears on the Desktop, the MP3 player can be safely disconnected from the USB port.

Check for iTunes Compatibility

1. To see if your MP3 player is compatible with iTunes, first check the player's documentation.

2. If the documentation is unclear, visit the Web site:

   ```
   docs.info.apple.com/article.html?
   artnum=93548
   ```

   This site lists some iTunes compatible players, as shown in Figure 13-2.

3. Visit the manufacturer's Web site for OS X downloads for your MP3 player.

    Although some third-party MP3 players may work with iTunes, keep in mind that unlike iPods — most other MP3 players — can't play AAC files. This means that songs purchased from the iTunes store won't work in most third-party MP3 players. For other music, convert it to MP3 format before copying it to a third-party MP3 player.

Figure 13-1: Third-party MP3 players should appear as Untitled volumes.

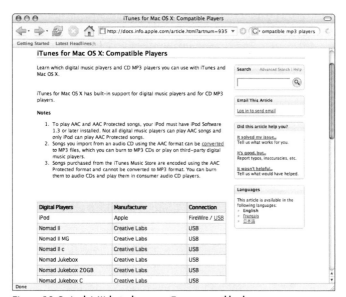

Figure 13-2: Apple's Web site lists some iTunes-compatible players.

Copy Music Files to the Player

1. Connect the MP3 player to your USB port.

2. Launch iTunes and arrange the windows so that you can see iTunes and the MP3 player icon at the same time, as shown in Figure 13-3.

3. Select the song or songs that you want to copy to the player.

 If you're not sure whether a song's format is compatible with your MP3 player, select the song in iTunes and press ⌘+I. An Info window opens, showing you information about the song, including the file format. MP3 files should be compatible with any MP3 player, but AAC files are usually compatible only with iPods.

4. Click and drag the songs to the MP3 player's icon, as shown in Figure 13-3. A progress window displays the file copying progress.

5. If you don't use iTunes to organize your music, use the Finder to copy files instead. Open a Finder window, browse to the file you want to copy to the MP3 player, and then click and drag the file to the MP3 player, as shown in Figure 13-4.

 You can also copy files from your MP3 player to your hard drive with the Finder; simply drag and drop files from the player to a hard drive folder to copy them. If some of the files are in WMA format, you must download and install Windows Media Player or Flip4Mac, as described in Chapter 14.

Figure 13-3: Click and drag songs from iTunes to your MP3 player.

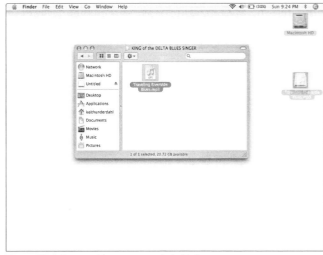

Figure 13-4: You can also copy music with the Finder.

Create Folders on the Player

1. Connect the MP3 player to your USB port and then double-click the player's icon to begin browsing it in the Finder.

2. If the files are disorganized and scattered all over the window — especially likely if the MP3 player has been used on a Windows PC — choose View⇨Clean Up, as shown in Figure 13-5.

3. To create a new folder, press ⌘+Shift+N or choose File⇨ New Folder.

4. Type a new name for the folder, as shown in Figure 13-6.

5. Use the Finder to copy files into the new folder, as described in the preceding section.

6. Unmount the MP3 player and disconnect it from the USB port.

7. Test the MP3 player to make sure that audio files placed in subfolders are recognized and play properly. Some MP3 players may not be able to play files that are placed in subfolders.

 Many MP3 players can be used as Thumb drives in a pinch. That is, if you have some files, such as PowerPoint presentations or Pages documents, and you need to quickly copy those files to another computer, you can copy the files to the storage area on an MP3 player and then connect the MP3 player to the other computer to retrieve the files.

Figure 13-5: Use the Finder to browse your MP3 player.

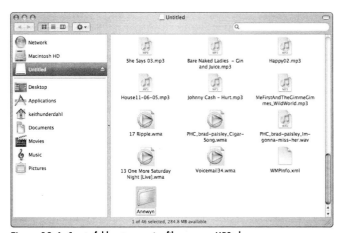

Figure 13-6: Create folders to organize files on your MP3 player.

Delete Files from the Player

1. Connect the MP3 player to your USB port and then double-click the player's icon to begin browsing it in the Finder.

2. Select a file or folder that you want to delete and then click and drag it to the Trash, as shown in Figure 13-7.

 To select multiple files or folders, hold down the ⌘ key and click each item that you want to select.

3. Press ⌘+Shift+Delete or choose Finder⇨Empty Trash.

4. Click OK to confirm that you want to empty the Trash, as shown in Figure 13-8.

 Make sure you empty the Trash before unmounting the MP3 player. If you leave Trash items on the MP3 player, the player may not play music properly and Windows users may have problems with the player's file system.

Figure 13-7: Drag files to the Trash to delete them.

Figure 13-8: Make sure you empty the Trash before unmounting the MP3 player.

Watching Videos and DVDs

A stroll around your local electronics store reveals a lot of cool digital gadgets, including TVs, stereo systems, and DVD players. Thankfully, you don't need any of those things because you have a Mac. Every new Macintosh comes with built-in DVD player hardware and software, and if you have a laptop, your Mac even doubles as a really nice portable DVD player.

Of course, DVDs aren't the only kinds of videos that you'll want to watch on your Mac. You may also download videos from the Internet or you may want to watch videos recorded by a digital camera or camera phone.

This chapter shows you how to watch DVDs on your Mac as well as how to watch other types of video. This chapter focuses on three specific programs:

- ➡ **DVD Player:** As the name implies, this is the program that allows your Mac to play movie DVDs.

- ➡ **QuickTime:** QuickTime is a popular program from Apple that allows you to watch videos in various formats, including MPEG and QuickTime video.

- ➡ **Flip4Mac:** This free program works as a plug-in for QuickTime and allows you to watch most Windows Media Video (WMV) on your Mac.

Change the Default DVD Player

1. Choose Apple⊅System Preferences (or open System Preferences from the Dock) and then click the CDs & DVDs icon to open CD & DVD preferences, as shown in Figure 14-1.

2. Make a selection in the When You Insert a Video DVD menu. The choices are

   - **Open DVD Player:** This is the default choice, and it is probably the best choice unless you prefer another third-party DVD player application.

   - **Open Front Row:** This is Leopard's multimedia interface. If your Mac has an Apple Remote, the remote's Menu button activates Front Row.

   - **Open Other Application:** Choose this to select a different application; then browse to an alternate DVD player, as shown in Figure 14-2, and click Choose.

   - **Run Script:** Choose this if you have a DVD-related AppleScript that you want to run when you insert DVDs.

   - **Ignore:** If you don't want anything to happen automatically when you insert a DVD, choose Ignore.

 Even if you choose Ignore, you can easily watch DVD movies by manually opening DVD Player from the Applications folder.

3. Close System Preferences after you make a selection.

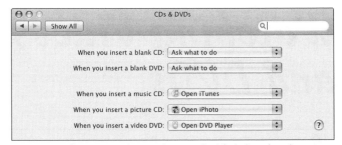

Figure 14-1: The OS X DVD Player application is the default choice for video DVDs.

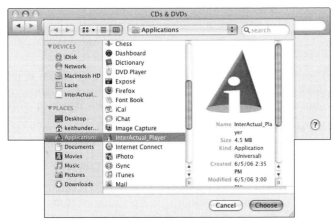

Figure 14-2: You can change the default DVD player if you wish.

Access DVD Features

1. Insert a movie DVD into your DVD drive. The DVD Player application starts automatically, and the movie plays.

2. If the movie opens in a small window, like the one shown in Figure 14-3, choose Video⇨Enter Full Screen or press ⌘+F. Press ⌘+F again to leave Full Screen mode.

3. Move the mouse pointer to the bottom of the screen to reveal the DVD Controller, as shown in Figure 14-4.

    If the Controller doesn't appear, hover the mouse pointer near the top of the screen and choose Window⇨Show Controller in the menu bar that appears.

4. Use the Play, Stop, Forward, and Back buttons to control playback. Click Menu or Title to open the DVD menu (the exact menu that opens varies, depending on the DVD) and use the arrow buttons to navigate DVD menus.

    Unless you have a tray-loading DVD drive (found only on Mac Pros, Power Macs, and some external drives), don't attempt to insert a 3.5" mini-DVD into your Mac's DVD drive. Mini-DVDs aren't compatible with the slot-loading drives found on iMacs, Mac Minis, and portable Macs.

Figure 14-3: The DVD Player can float over your desktop, just like other applications.

Figure 14-4: Use the controls to take command of DVD features.

Modify DVD Player Settings

1. Open the DVD Player application.

2. Choose DVD Player⇨Preferences. If the menu bar is hidden, hover the mouse pointer near the top of the screen.

3. In the Player screen, choose whether you want DVD Player to open automatically in Full Screen mode and start playing when you insert a disc.

4. Click Disc Setup and select default languages, as shown in Figure 14-5. If you're using external audio speakers, select the speakers in the Audio Output menu.

 If you're using System Sound Output on a laptop, don't place a check mark next to Disable Dolby Dynamic Range Compression. Disabling this option could damage your laptop's small speakers.

5. Click Full Screen and choose how long you want to wait before the Controller disappears.

6. Click Windows and change the appearance of Closed Captioning text if you wish.

7. Click Previously Viewed and select a default behavior for previously viewed DVDs.

8. If your Mac has a High Definition (HD) compatible DVD player, click High Definition and choose a picture height that matches your display, as shown in Figure 14-6.

9. Click OK to close the Preferences window.

 If you see horizontal lines in the video during playback (especially on fast-moving subjects), choose Video⇨Deinterlace to enable or disable interlacing. Deinterlacing is often necessary when watching video DVDs on non-interlaced displays, such as computer monitors.

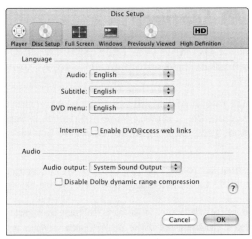

Figure 14-5: Select default languages for DVD Player.

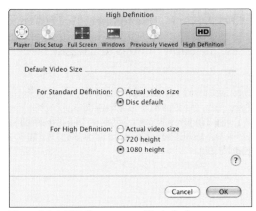

Figure 14-6: DVD Player supports HD playback.

Watch Movies with QuickTime

1. Launch QuickTime by clicking its icon on the Dock or double-click the QuickTime icon in the Applications folder.

    If you double-click a movie that is compatible with QuickTime — compatible formats include MPEG and QT — QuickTime launches automatically and plays the video.

2. To open a movie, choose File➪Open File.

3. In the Open window that appears (as shown in Figure 14-7), browse to the movie you want to view.

4. Select the movie file and click Open. If the movie is in a format that isn't supported by QuickTime, an error message appears advising you of this fact.

5. Use the playback controls to play the movie, as shown in Figure 14-8.

    For advanced playback controls, choose Window➪Show A/V Controls. The A/V Controls allow you to adjust color, light, contrast, audio characteristics, and playback speed.

    To change the size of the video image, open the View menu and choose Half Size, Actual Size, Double Size, or Fit to Screen. You can also click and drag the bottom-right corner of the QuickTime window to dynamically resize it.

    QuickTime offers an online content guide with links to movie trailers, music videos, and other entertainments. To open the content guide, open QuickTime and choose Window➪Show Content Guide.

Figure 14-7: Locate the movie you want to view.

Figure 14-8: QuickTime offers a simple, friendly interface.

Adjust QuickTime Settings

1. Open QuickTime and choose QuickTime Player⇨ Preferences.

2. In the Preferences window, as shown in Figure 14-9, adjust general QuickTime Preferences as follows:

   • If you don't want to spawn a new window every time you open another movie, deselect Open Movies in New Players.

   • Deselect Show Equalizer if you find the graphic equalizer display distracting.

   • If you don't want the Content Guide to appear when you open QuickTime, deselect Show Content Guide Automatically.

 For additional QuickTime settings, click the QuickTime icon in System Preferences. There you can change disk cache settings (the cache is where downloaded movies are stored) and other basic QuickTime characteristics.

Update QuickTime

1. Open QuickTime and choose QuickTime Player⇨Update Existing Software.

2. In the Software Update window that appears, as shown in Figure 14-10, review available updates.

3. If a QuickTime update is available, select it and click Install.

 For more on using Software Update, see Chapter 4.

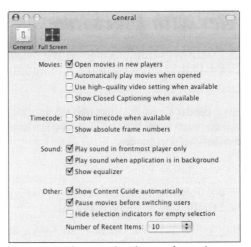

Figure 14-9: Adjust general QuickTime preferences here.

Figure 14-10: Use Software Update to check for QuickTime updates.

Install Flip4Mac

1. Visit www.flip4mac.com, click the Download link, and then click the Flip4Mac WMV link.

2. Click the Get WMV Player Free link.

3. When you're redirected to the Microsoft Web site, click the Free Download link. Read any instructions that appear and click Download.

4. If you see the file download dialog, select Save to Disk and click OK.

5. When the download is complete, double-click the downloaded disk image (the icon has .dmg at the end of the file name).

 If you use Safari to download Flip4Mac, Step 5 is unnecessary because the disk image mounts automatically.

6. If the Flip4Mac WMV disk image doesn't open automatically, double-click its icon on the Desktop.

7. Double-click the Flip4Mac installer package and follow the instructions onscreen to install, as shown in Figure 14-11. When you get to the Installation Type screen, click Customize to select options, as shown in Figure 14-12.

8. Click Install to begin installation and click Close when installation is complete.

 If you have Microsoft Windows Media Player for OS X installed on your computer, upgrade to Flip4Mac. Microsoft no longer supports Windows Media Player for OS X, so it doesn't play the latest Windows Media formats.

Figure 14-11: Save the download file to disk.

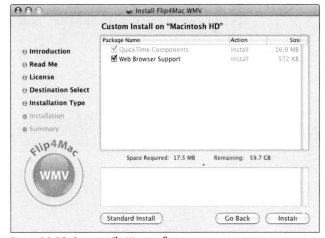

Figure 14-12: Customize Flip4Mac installation options.

View Windows Media Video with Flip4Mac

1. To open a Windows Media file, either

   - **Double-click a Windows Media file.** (Windows Media Audio has the .wma file name extension, and Windows Media Video has the .wmv file name extension.)

   - **Open QuickTime and choose File⇨Open to locate a Windows Media file, as shown in Figure 14-13.**

2. Use the playback controls to play the Windows Media Video in QuickTime, as shown in Figure 14-14.

 If you want to edit Windows Media Video in iMovie or QuickTime, play Windows Media in your iPod, or convert Windows Media to other formats, you can purchase WMV Player Pro from Flip4Mac for $29. Other versions are also available; click the WMV Products link on the Flip4Mac Web site to discover more.

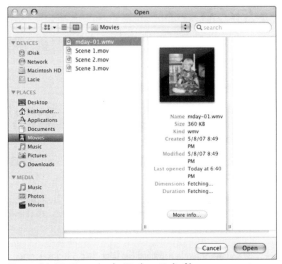

Figure 14-13: Browse to the Windows Media file you want to view.

Figure 14-14: Flip4Mac lets QuickTime view Windows Media.

Viewing, Organizing, and Improving Pictures

*I*t's hard to imagine now how anyone ever got by without digital cameras. Back in the days of film cameras, photo processing was expensive and slow, and if you wanted to improve the quality of your photos, you had to just shoot a lot of (expensive) pictures and become a better photographer.

A digital camera won't make you a great photographer, but it will definitely make your life easier. Not only can you snap many photos without worrying about processing fees, but you can quickly copy your digital images to your computer where they can be easily reshaped, retouched, and shared with others via e-mail or the Internet.

This chapter shows you how to organize your photos with iPhoto, a program included free with your Mac. In addition to organizing photos, iPhoto can also make basic edits and improvements to photos. This chapter also introduces you to Adobe Photoshop Elements, a slightly more advanced photo editing program available for less than $100 for your Mac at most Apple and computer retailers.

 If you need an online home for sharing your digital photos with others over the Internet, check out Chapter 9.

Launch iPhoto

1. To launch iPhoto, either click the iPhoto icon on the Dock (the iPhoto icon looks like a camera in front of a picture) or open the Applications folder and double-click iPhoto.

2. If you're launching iPhoto for the first time, you're asked if you want to use iPhoto when you connect a digital camera to the computer, as shown in Figure 15-1. Click a button to make a choice.

3. If you see an iPhoto Update window, click Learn More to download the update or click Cancel if you don't want to update at this time.

To quickly check for iPhoto updates, open iPhoto and then choose iPhoto➪Check for Updates.

Figure 15-1: Decide whether you want iPhoto to work with your digital camera.

Download Photos from a Camera

1. Connect your digital camera to your computer's Universal Serial Bus (USB) port and then turn on the camera.

2. When iPhoto switches to Import mode, as shown in Figure 15-2, type a name and description for the roll.

If iPhoto doesn't switch automatically to Import mode, make sure your digital camera is turned on and in Photo Viewing mode. If the camera is in Picture Taking mode, iPhoto can't import photos from it.

3. Click Import to begin importing photos from your camera.

To import pictures that are already on your hard drive, choose File➪Add to Library. Use the Finder to find and import photos.

Figure 15-2: Enter a roll name and click Import.

Organize Your Photo Library

1. Launch iPhoto and then click Library in the Source pane on the left side of the screen to view your entire Photo Library, as shown in Figure 15-3.

2. To create a new album in which to organize certain pictures, choose File⇨New Album and then type a descriptive name for the album.

3. Click and drag photos from the Library window to the new album. In Figure 15-4, a new album named Brownsville was created.

To copy multiple photos, first click and drag a box around all the photos you want to move. Alternatively, hold down the ⌘ key and click individual pictures that you want to select. When a group is selected, you can then click and drag that group to a new album.

4. Click the name of an album to view its contents, as shown in Figure 15-4.

5. To change the size of photo thumbnails, click and drag the Zoom slider in the lower-right corner of the iPhoto screen. In Figure 15-4, the thumbnail size was increased.

6. To display file names for photos, as shown in Figure 15-4, choose View⇨Titles.

You can also choose to display keywords, film rolls, and ratings from the View menu.

7. To delete a photo, simply drag it to the Trash icon in the Source pane on the left side of the iPhoto screen.

Figure 15-3: Click Library to view all your photos.

Figure 15-4: Organize your photos into albums.

Rotate Photos

1. Locate an image that you want to rotate and double-click the image to open it in the Editing window, as shown in Figure 15-5.

2. Click the Rotate button at the bottom of the Editing window to rotate the image.

 You may need to click Rotate a couple times to get the desired orientation.

3. Click Done to save your changes.

Resize Images

1. Select a photo that you want to export in a smaller size.

2. Choose Share⊅Export.

3. Select Scale Images No Larger Than and enter a maximum width and/or height, as shown in Figure 15-6.

4. Click Export.

5. Enter a new file name, choose a location for the resized image, and click OK.

 Most Internet users don't have nice, big Apple displays, so the two most common screen resolutions for Internet users are 1024 x 768 and 800 x 600. Because of this, resize images you plan to share online so that they can be viewed easily at these resolutions.

Figure 15-5: Images can be easily rotated.

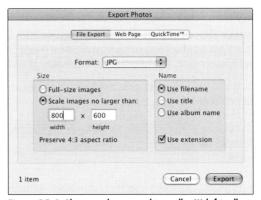

Figure 15-6: Photos can be exported in smaller, Web-friendly sizes.

Crop Images

1. Locate the image you want to crop and click it once to select it.

2. Choose Photos➪Duplicate to create a copy of the image.

3. Double-click the copy to open it in the Editing window.

4. Click and drag a rectangle over the area of the photo that you want to keep, as shown in Figure 15-7. Areas outside the rectangle will be cropped.

 It's best to start with a relatively large image; if you crop smaller images, the resulting cropped image may be too small.

5. Click the Crop button on the toolbar at the bottom of the Editing window, as shown in Figure 15-8.

6. After you're done editing the image, click Done to close the Editing window.

 If you don't like the changes you've made to an image, select the image in your Library and choose Photos➪Revert to Original.

Figure 15-7: Select the cropping area.

Figure 15-8: Click Crop to crop the image.

Create a Slideshow

1. Open iPhoto and select a picture roll or album from which you want to base your slideshow.

2. Click Slideshow near the bottom of the iPhoto window. A new slideshow is created, as shown in Figure 15-9, and it contains all the images in the roll or album you selected in Step 1.

3. To remove an image from the slideshow, click and drag it to the Trash icon in the Source pane.

4. To add photos from other albums or rolls, simply click and drag the photos to the desired slideshow in the Source pane.

 To change the order of images, click and drag their thumbnails left or right at the top of the Slideshow window.

5. Click a photo in the slideshow and then choose None, Black and White, or Sepia from the Effect menu to change that photo.

6. Choose a transition to use between photos in the Transitions menu or choose the default Dissolve transition.

7. Place a check mark next to Ken Burns Effect to create a subtle zooming effect on your images.

8. To change the display time for each photo, click Settings and enter a new time, as shown in Figure 15-10. Click OK to close the Settings window.

9. Click Play to play the slideshow. To stop the slideshow, simply click anywhere on an image during the show.

 To add a musical soundtrack to your slideshow, click Music and then choose a song or playlist from your iTunes Library.

Figure 15-9: Quickly create slideshows based on your rolls or albums.

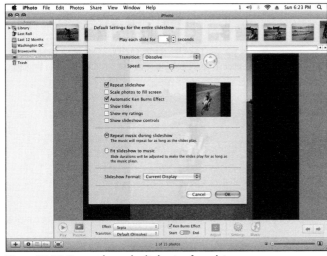

Figure 15-10: You can change the display time for each image.

Install Adobe Photoshop Elements

1. Quit all open applications and then insert the Adobe Photoshop Elements installation CD into your disc drive.

2. Double-click the disc's icon to open the Disc window.

3. Double-click the Install Adobe Photoshop Elements icon, as shown in Figure 15-11, and follow the instructions onscreen to accept the license agreement and complete installation.

    Remember, you'll need an administrator's name and password to install the software.

4. Restart your computer when you're prompted to do so. You can safely eject the Adobe installation disc after the restart.

5. Open the Applications folder and then double-click the Adobe Photoshop Elements folder to open it.

6. Double-click the Photoshop Elements icon and then choose an option in the Welcome screen, as shown in Figure 15-12. The options are

   - **Start from Scratch:** Choose this if you just want to open Elements without opening an image file.

   - **Browse with Adobe Bridge:** Choose this to browse to an image file. Adobe Bridge is similar to the Apple Finder, but with picture browsing features similar to iPhoto.

   - **Import from Camera or Scanner:** This choice helps you quickly import images from a camera or scanner.

   - **Recent Images:** Click the name of a recently edited image (if any are listed) to re-open the image.

    To add Photoshop Elements to the Dock, click and drag the Application icon to the Dock.

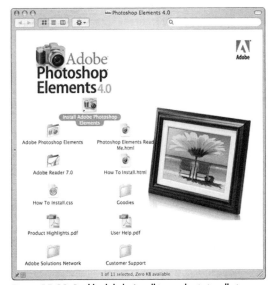

Figure 15-11: Double-click the Install icon to begin installation.

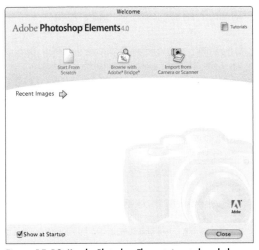

Figure 15-12: Use the Photoshop Elements icon to launch the program.

Resize an Image in Adobe Photoshop

1. Open an image file with Adobe Bridge.

    If you don't like using Adobe Bridge, open Photoshop and simply choose File⇨Open. You can then browse to files with the Finder instead of Adobe Bridge.

2. Choose Image⇨Resize⇨Image Size, as shown in Figure 15-13.

3. In the Image Size dialog that appears, place a check mark next to Resample Image, as shown in Figure 15-14.

4. Enter a new size with pixel dimensions in the upper half of the Image Size dialog, as shown in Figure 15-14, or enter a new document size in the lower half of the dialog.

    If you're resizing the image for Web or computer screen use, change the pixel dimensions. If you're resizing the image for later printing, use the document size section. If the image will be printed, change the resolution to 300 pixels per inch before reducing the document size. This ensures the best possible print quality.

    In most cases, leave Constrain Proportions checked. If you deselect this option, the image appears distorted after resizing.

5. Click OK.

    To crop an image, click and drag a box on the image and choose Image⇨Crop.

    When you crop or reduce the size of an image, make sure you choose File⇨Save As and save the file with a different file name. If you save the original file, you'll lose some of the original image quality and you can never get it back.

Figure 15-13: Choose Image⇨Resize⇨Image Size to begin resizing.

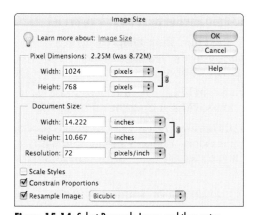

Figure 15-14: Select Resample Image and then enter a new size.

Improve Color with Photoshop

1. Open the image that you want to improve.

2. Choose File⇨Save As and save a copy of the image using a new file name. In the Save As dialog, choose Photoshop in the Format menu.

3. Open the Enhance menu, as shown in Figure 15-15, and then choose something that you want to improve. The choices are

   - **Auto Smart Fix:** Quickly make common image adjustments

   - **Auto Levels:** Fine-tunes color, light, and contrast

   - **Auto Contrast:** Improves contrast and light

   - **Auto Color Correction:** Adjusts and improves color

   - **Auto Red Eye Fix:** Removes red dots from subjects' eyes

 No single enhancement will improve every image. If you don't like the changes made by an enhancement, press ⌘+Z to undo the change and then try a different enhancement.

4. To fine-tune light and contrast, choose Enhance⇨Adjust Lighting⇨Brightness/Contrast. Use the sliders to make fine adjustments and preview the changes in the background. Click OK to accept your changes or click Cancel to reject them.

5. To fine-tune color, choose Enhance⇨Adjust Color⇨ Color Variations. Click sample images to choose variations, as shown in Figure 15-16. Click OK to accept your changes or click Cancel to reject them.

Figure 15-15: Use the Enhance menu to make quick image enhancements.

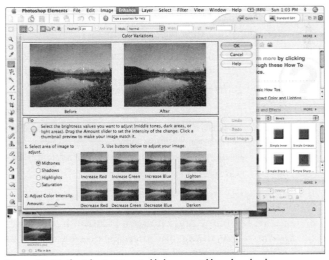

Figure 15-16: The Color Variations tool helps you quickly make color changes.

Export a Photoshop Image for the Web

1. After you're done enhancing and improving an image, choose File⇨Save for Web, as shown in Figure 15-17.

2. In the Save for Web window that appears, as shown in Figure 15-18, choose a preset format in the Preset menu on the right.

> The GIF format is better for smaller images that have less color. Larger photos should be saved in JPEG format. The PNG format offers good quality but limited compatibility with some Web browsers (notably, Internet Explorer 6 and older).

3. Choose sub-options below the Preset menu, such as quality levels.

4. Enter a new size for the image in the Width and Height fields below New Size, as shown in Figure 15-18.

5. After entering a new size, click Apply.

6. Note the file size listed below the image preview on the right side of the Save for Web preview window. This will be the approximate file size of the image when you export it.

> Pay careful attention to the file size and estimated download time for the image. Remember, many people still have relatively slow dial-up Internet connections, so they'll have a hard time viewing large image files.

7. Click OK.

8. Enter a file name and choose a location in the Save Optimized As dialog and then click Save to save the file.

Figure 15-17: Choose File⇨Save for Web to save a Web image.

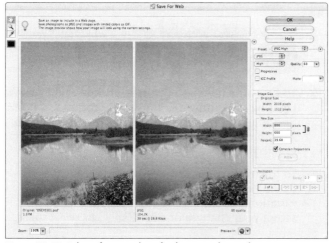

Figure 15-18: Select a format and size for the exported image here.

Making Movies

Apple has been a pioneer in digital video for over a decade. In the 1990s, Apple helped develop the *IEEE-1394 FireWire interface*, a high-speed data bus that allows high-quality digital video to be transferred quickly between digital camcorders and computers. Apple also pioneered software that helps you turn your raw video footage into a great movie with titles, music, and special effects.

Every new Macintosh computer comes with a FireWire port and iMovie pre-installed. The iMovie application allows you to import video from a digital camcorder, assemble a movie with only the scenes you want, add sound and video effects to your movie clips, and export your finished movie for viewing over the Internet or back to videotape. And if your Mac has a SuperDrive, you can also burn your movie straight to DVD.

This chapter shows you how to make movies with your digital camcorder and iMovie. Tasks show you how to create a new movie project, capture video from your camcorder, and turn your footage into a great movie. Tasks also show you how to export your finished movie in a Web-friendly format or burn it to DVD.

 When buying a new camcorder, avoid cameras that use DVDs or mini DVDs as their recording medium. DVD-based camcorders often lack FireWire ports and usually aren't Mac-compatible. Digital camcorders that use MiniDV tapes and have FireWire ports are always Mac-compatible, and they offer the best balance of quality and value. For more on making movies and working with iMovie, check out *Digital Video For Dummies, 4th Edition*, by Keith Underdahl (Wiley Publishing, Inc.).

Chapter 16

Get ready to . . .

Launch iMovie

1. Click the iMovie HD icon on the Dock or double-click the iMovie HD icon in the Applications folder.

    You can also open iMovie by double-clicking an iMovie project file.

2. Choose an option in the window, as shown in Figure 16-1. The options include

   • **Create a New Project:** Choose this to create a new movie from scratch. When you create a new project, provide a name for the new project, as shown in Figure 16-2. You can also choose a different format by clicking the arrow next to Video Format and choosing a different format, as shown in Figure 16-2.

    The selection in the Video Format menu should match the format recorded by your camera. Most consumer MiniDV cameras use the DV format. If you're importing video, the Video Format menu should match the format of the file you wish to import.

   • **Open an Existing Project:** Choose this to open a movie that you worked on and saved. A dialog box opens allowing you to browse to your movie project file.

   • **Make a Magic iMovie:** Choose this to let iMovie automatically create a movie for you. Make sure your camcorder is connected to your computer's FireWire port and turned on to Player or VTR mode before choosing the Magic iMovie option.

Figure 16-1: Choose what you want to do here.

 To quickly open a recent project while working in iMovie, choose File➪Open Recent.

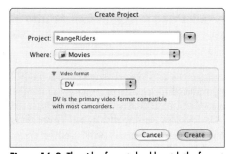

Figure 16-2: The video format should match the format of your camcorder.

Capture Video from a Camcorder

1. Launch iMovie and create a new project, as described in the preceding section.

2. Connect your camcorder to your computer's FireWire port and make sure that the camcorder is turned on to Player or VTR mode.

    Some camcorders may use a different name for the FireWire port, such as DV, IEEE-1394, or i.Link.

3. In iMovie, move the control switch from Edit to Import.

    The control switch is located below the main Preview window, and has a camera icon on one side and a scissors icon on the other. Move this switch to the camera icon to capture video, or to the scissor icon to edit your movie.

4. When the Preview screen turns blue and says Camera Connected, as shown in Figure 16-3, click the Play button to start playing the tape in the camcorder.

5. Use the playback controls to play, pause, fast forward, and rewind the video to find scenes that you want to capture.

6. Rewind to slightly before the second of video that you want to capture and then click the Import button on the Preview screen. Captured video clips appear in the Clips pane, as shown in Figure 16-4.

7. Click Stop when you're done capturing.

    To change the way iMovie captures video, choose iMovie HD⇨Preferences and then click Import. There you can choose whether clips are created automatically and other settings.

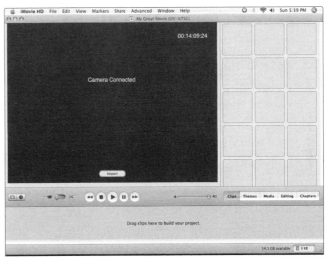

Figure 16-3: The camera is connected, and iMovie is ready to capture video.

Figure 16-4: Captured video clips are stored in the Clips pane.

Assemble Clips into a Movie

1. Open a movie project with captured video, as described earlier in this chapter.

2. If iMovie isn't already in Editing mode, move the Control slider to Edit (it looks like scissors).

3. Click a clip in the Clips pane and then click Play below the Preview window to play the clip.

4. If you want to split a clip in half, pause playback at the point where you want to split the clip and then choose Edit⊅Split Video Clip at Playhead, as shown in Figure 16-5.

5. Click and drag video clips from the Clips pane to the Clip Viewer at the bottom of the screen, as shown in Figure 16-6.

 If the bottom of your iMovie screen doesn't look like the examples shown here, you probably have the Timeline shown instead of the Clip Viewer. Choose View⊅Switch to Clip Viewer to switch to the Clip Viewer. The Clip Viewer is the same thing as a storyboard, which is the term used by many other video editing programs.

6. To change the order of clips in the Clip Viewer, simply click and drag the clips back and forth to new positions.

7. To remove a clip from the movie, click and drag it back to the Clips Pane.

 If you drag clips to the Trash bin located in the lower-right corner of the iMovie window, those clips are deleted from your hard drive the next time the Trash is emptied. The iMovie Trash is emptied every time you quit iMovie. If you want to use deleted clips in the future, they must be re-captured from the video tape.

Figure 16-5: Split clips for easier editing.

Figure 16-6: Click and drag clips to the Clip Viewer.

Trim Clips on the Timeline

1. Open a movie project in which you've already added some clips to the Clip Viewer, as described in the preceding section.

2. To switch from the Clip Viewer to the Timeline, as shown in Figure 16-7, choose View⇨Switch to Timeline Viewer or click the Timeline button below the lower-left corner of the Preview window.

    The Timeline button has a clock on it.

    To adjust the zoom level of the Timeline, use the Zoom slider in the lower-left corner of the iMovie screen.

3. Click in the Timeline and then click Play to play the Timeline.

4. When you identify a clip that you want to trim, pause playback so that the playhead is exactly on the spot to which you want to trim.

   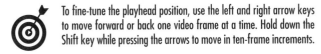 To fine-tune the playhead position, use the left and right arrow keys to move forward or back one video frame at a time. Hold down the Shift key while pressing the arrows to move in ten-frame increments.

5. Click and drag the edge of the clip until it meets the playhead, as shown in Figure 16-8. Other clips in the Timeline automatically move over to fill in the space made by a trimmed clip.

Figure 16-7: Switch iMovie to Timeline view for precision editing.

Figure 16-8: Click and drag the edge of a clip to trim it.

Add a Soundtrack

1. Open an iMovie project that's been edited, as described earlier in this chapter.

    If the song you want to use for your soundtrack isn't already on your computer, use iTunes to import the song from an audio CD or the iTunes Music Store, as described in Chapter 12.

2. In iMovie, click the Media button below the Clips pane on the right side of the screen.

3. Click iTunes in the Media list to view your iTunes Library, as shown in Figure 16-9.

    Click the arrow next to iTunes to browse specific iTunes playlists.

4. Click a song to select it and then click the Play button below the Media list to preview the song.

5. In the Timeline, move the playhead to the place where you want the song to begin.

    Press the Home key to quickly move the playhead to the beginning of the movie.

6. Click and drag a song to the Timeline to add it to your movie. The song should be dropped on one of the audio tracks below the main video track, as shown in Figure 16-10.

7. Choose View➪Show Clip Volume Levels to reveal the audio volume rubber bands on the audio clips. Click and drag on points of the rubber bands, as shown in Figure 16-10, to adjust audio volume.

Figure 16-9: Browse your iTunes Library for soundtrack music.

Figure 16-10: Use the volume rubber bands to adjust volume.

Insert Sound Effects

1. Open an iMovie project that's been edited, as described earlier in this chapter.

2. In iMovie, click the Media button below the Clips pane on the right side of the screen.

3. Click Standard Sound Effects or Skywalker Sound Effects in the Media list to view your iTunes Library, as shown in Figure 16-11.

 You may have other available sound effects categories, such as iLife Sound Effects. Spend some time browsing your sound effects library to find out what's available.

4. Double-click a sound effect to hear a preview.

5. In the Timeline, move the playhead to the place where you want to insert the sound effect.

6. Click and drag the sound effect to the Timeline, as shown in Figure 16-12, or click Place at Playhead.

7. Choose View➪Show Clip Volume Levels to reveal the audio volume rubber bands on the audio clips. Click and drag on points of the rubber bands to adjust audio volume.

 iMovie also lets you record your own narration. If your Mac doesn't have a built-in microphone, connect a microphone to the Mic port, or connect a USB mic to the USB port. Place the playhead at the place where you want to begin recording narration and then click the Record button in the lower-right corner of the Media pane. The Microphone graph lights up when you record audio. Click the Record button again to stop recording.

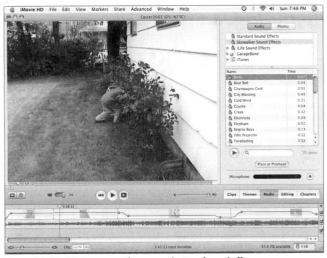

Figure 16-11: iMovie comes with a great selection of sound effects.

Figure 16-12: Click and drag the sound effect to the Timeline.

Apply Video Effects

1. Open an iMovie project that's been edited, as described earlier in this chapter.

2. In iMovie, click the Editing button below the Clips pane on the right side of the screen and then click Video FX at the top of the Editing pane to reveal a list of video effects, as shown in Figure 16-13.

3. In the Timeline, click a video clip to which you want to apply a video effect.

4. Click the name of a video effect to preview it, as shown in Figure 16-14.

    When you preview an effect, the preview plays over and over in the Preview window. Click the Stop (X) button in the Preview window to stop the effect preview.

5. Use the controls in the lower half of the Editing pane to adjust features of the effect. The exact controls available vary, depending on the selected effect.

6. To apply the effect, click Apply. The application process — *rendering* — may take a few minutes, depending on the clip length, the effect complexity, and the computer speed.

    You can apply multiple video effects to a clip. After applying one clip, select and apply another clip.

7. To remove effects from a video clip, click the clip to select it and then choose Advanced⇨Revert Clip to Original.

Figure 16-13: Browse video effects in the Editing pane.

Figure 16-14: Preview and adjust the effects before applying them.

Insert Transitions between Clips

1. Open an iMovie project that's been edited, as described earlier in this chapter.

2. In iMovie, click the Editing button below the Clips pane on the right side of the screen and then click Transitions to reveal a list of video effects, as shown in Figure 16-15.

3. In the Timeline, click a video clip to which you want to apply a transition.

4. Click the name of a transition to preview it.

5. Adjust the Speed slider to change the speed of the transition, if desired.

 Some transitions are directional. Use the directional buttons next to the Speed slider to change the direction of directional transitions.

6. Click and drag the transition to a spot between clips in the Timeline, as shown in Figure 16-16.

7. To remove a transition, click the transition in the Timeline and press Delete.

 For best results, use transitions sparingly and conservatively. Transitions should be used only between major scene changes, not between every single clip. Choose transitions that don't distract from the actual video content of your movie. Also, be aware that transitions sometimes add time to your movie, which can become troublesome if you have a carefully timed soundtrack.

Figure 16-15: Transitions are a nice addition between some clips.

Figure 16-16: Click and drag transitions to the Timeline.

Add Titles to Your Movie

1. Open an iMovie project that's been edited, as described earlier in this chapter.

2. In iMovie, click the Editing button below the Clips pane on the right side of the screen and then click Titles to reveal a list of title styles.

3. In the Timeline, click a video clip to which you want to apply a transition. Make sure that the playhead is positioned where you want the title to first appear in the movie.

4. Click the name of a title style to preview it.

5. In the text boxes below the title styles list, enter the text for your title, as shown in Figure 16-17.

 Use the formatting menus to change the font, style, and size of the text. Sans serif fonts, such as Arial, work best in video; serif fonts, like Times New Roman, can cause flickering on some TV screens.

6. To make your titles float over a video image rather than a black screen, deselect Over Black, as shown in Figure 16-18.

7. Adjust the duration of the title with the Speed slider near the bottom of the Editing pane.

 Some titles fade in and out. Use the Pause slider to adjust the fading speed.

8. Click the Add button to add the title to your movie.

Figure 16-17: Choose a title style and then enter some text.

Figure 16-18: Deselect the Over Black option to float your titles over video.

Export the Movie for Web Viewing

1. Complete all edits for your movie, as described earlier in this chapter.

2. Choose Share➪QuickTime.

3. Choose a format in the Compress Movie For menu, as shown in Figure 16-19. Notice that a file size estimate and other format details are listed for the format you choose.

    Many Web users still can't or won't download large files. The smaller the file size, the more likely it is that more people will see your movie.

4. If you want to fine-tune Export settings, choose Expert Settings in the Compress Movie For menu and then click Share.

5. If you choose Expert Settings, choose a format in the Use menu, as shown in Figure 16-20.

    If you're familiar with frame rates, video sizes, and other advanced video topics, click Options to fine-tune your Export settings. In most cases, it is safest to use just one of the preset formats provided by iMovie.

6. Provide a file name for your movie and choose a location in which to save it in the Where menu.

    For online movies, don't use spaces in the file name and make sure that the .mov file name extension remains intact.

7. Click Save to save your file. The export process may take a few minutes, depending on the length of your movie and complexity of your edits.

Figure 16-19: Higher quality means bigger file sizes.

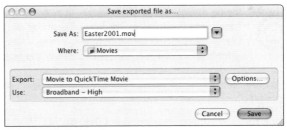

Figure 16-20: Name and save your movie.

Burn the Movie to DVD

1. Complete all edits for your movie, as described earlier in this chapter, and choose File⇨Save Project to save your movie.

2. Choose Share⇨iDVD.

    To create a movie that can play in common home DVD players, make sure you follow the steps here and don't choose File⇨Burn Project to Disc. Discs created with the Burn Project to Disc feature aren't compatible with standard DVD players.

3. In the iDVD tab that appears, click Share.

4. When iDVD launches, click a DVD theme to preview it. If you're asked whether you want to change the aspect ratio of your movie or keep it, as shown in Figure 16-21, click Keep.

    Use the menu at the top of the Themes list to view additional themes. Some themes include Drop Zones where you can drop pictures or video clips. Click Menu in the lower-right corner of the iDVD screen to place photos from your iPhoto library into Drop Zones.

5. Double-click a line of text in the DVD menu to change the text.

6. Click the Burn button or choose File⇨Burn DVD.

7. When you're prompted to enter a recordable DVD, as shown in Figure 16-22, insert a blank disc. The encoding and recording process may take several hours.

Figure 16-21: iDVD includes some nice DVD themes.

Figure 16-22: Insert a recordable DVD.

Part 5
Networking Your Mac

The 5th Wave   By Rich Tennant

"Okay, a patient is admitted with a comatose Blackberry, a beeping pager, and a failing iPod-what do you do?! Think! Think!"

Networking Wirelessly with AirPort

Next to the World Wide Web, few technologies have revolutionized personal computing in recent years as much as wireless networking. With Apple's emphasis on ease-of-use, it comes as no surprise that Macs were among the first computers to take advantage of networking with no strings attached.

AirPort is Apple's name for its wireless networking products. AirPort gear is fully compatible with most other 802.11 (also sometimes called Wi-Fi) wireless networking technologies. Thus, your AirPort-equipped MacBook can access the Internet through public hotspots, and Wi-Fi-equipped Windows PCs can connect to your Apple AirPort access point.

This chapter shows you how to configure an AirPort access point to create your own wireless network. It also shows you how to connect your computers — both Windows PCs and Macs — to a wireless access point. This chapter also shows you how to create a wireless ad hoc computer-to-computer network.

 The steps for connecting a computer (whether a Mac or Windows PC) to a wireless access point are the same regardless of whether the access point is an Apple AirPort unit or another type of Wi-Fi access point. See Chapter 20 for more on setting up wireless network security. For even more on wireless networking, check out Michael E. Cohen's *AirPort and Mac Wireless Networks For Dummies* (Wiley Publishing, Inc.).

Get ready to . . .

Configure an AirPort Base Station

1. Connect an Ethernet cable between your broadband modem and the AirPort Base Station, if needed.

    See the owner's manual that comes with your Base Station for more information on cable connections. Whatever cables you connect, the power cord should be the last cable you connect.

2. Plug in the power cable for the Base Station and wait until the status light turns solid green.

3. Open the Applications folder on your Mac and then open the Utilities subfolder.

4. Double-click the AirPort Utility icon, as shown in Figure 17-1.

5. If your AirPort Base Station appears on the left, select it and then click Continue. Otherwise, choose Set Up a New AirPort Base Station, and click Continue.

6. When the Base Station is detected, click Continue.

    If the Base Station isn't detected, make sure that AirPort is enabled on your Mac and make sure that the status light on the Base Station is shining solid green. If the light is amber or is flashing, wait a few more seconds. If after a minute it still doesn't shine solid green, unplug the Base Station for a few seconds and then plug it back in. When the light shines solid green, click Try Again in the AirPort Setup Assistant.

7. Choose whether you want to create a new wireless network, as shown in Figure 17-2, or connect the Base Station to your existing wireless network.

Figure 17-1: Launch the AirPort Utility from the Applications:Utilities folder.

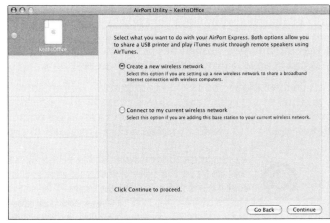

Figure 17-2: Set up a new AirPort Base Station.

8. Click Continue and then enter names for Wireless Network and the Base Station, as shown in Figure 17-3.

 If you're adding the Base Station to an existing network, the Wireless Network Name should be the same as the rest of your network. If you're creating a new network, enter a unique, personalized name for the network. Make sure that the Base Station's name is also descriptive, especially if you have more than one Base Station. This name makes it easier to identify and manage the device later.

9. Click Continue and choose a security format, as shown in Figure 17-4.

 WPA (Wi-Fi Protected Access) is the best type of security, but older computers and devices (such as game consoles) may support only WEP (Wired Equivalency Protocol). Use the highest level of security that's supported by the equipment you own. See Chapter 20 for more on wireless network security.

10. Click Continue and choose whether the AirPort Base Station connects to a router or modem.

11. Click Continue and choose how you connect to the Internet. In most cases, you want to choose the first option, which utilizes Dynamic Host Configuration Protocol (DHCP).

12. Enter a password for the Base Station. Keep this password safe because you'll need it to make changes to the Base Station later.

13. Click Continue, verify the setup details, and click Update.

14. After the Base Station restarts and the Congratulations screen appears, click Quit. Setup is complete.

 The steps described here are the same whether you have an AirPort Express or AirPort Extreme Base Station.

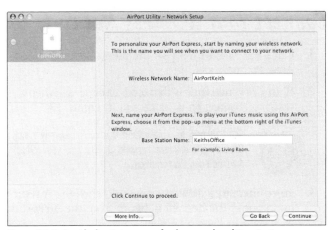

Figure 17-3: Provide descriptive names for the network and Base Station.

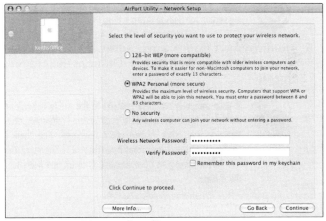

Figure 17-4: Use WPA security, if possible.

Connect to a Wireless Network

1. Click the AirPort icon on the menu bar and choose Turn AirPort On.

2. If an open network is detected, choose whether you want to connect to it, as shown in Figure 17-5.

    Don't connect to a network if you can't positively identify it. Connecting to unknown networks could expose your computer to data theft and virus infection.

3. To connect to a different network, click the AirPort icon and choose the desired network from the AirPort menu, as shown in Figure 17-6.

    If the desired network isn't listed, the network might not be in range, it might be turned off, or it might be closed. See the following section for steps to access a closed network.

4. To disconnect from a wireless network, click the AirPort icon and choose Turn AirPort Off from the AirPort menu.

    If your computer routinely connects to the wrong network when multiple networks are available, open System Preferences, click the Network icon, click AirPort, click Advanced, and then click Configure. In the If No Recent Networks Are Found menu, choose Ask Before Joining an Open Network. Click OK and Apply to save the change.

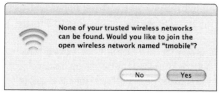

Figure 17-5: Choose whether you want to connect to the new network.

Figure 17-6: Choose a different network from the AirPort menu.

Access a Closed Wireless Network

1. Turn on AirPort if it isn't enabled already.

 Remember, you can use the AirPort menu to quickly turn AirPort on or off.

2. Click the AirPort icon in the menu bar and then choose Other from the menu that appears, as shown in Figure 17-7.

3. Enter the name of the network in the Network Name field.

 The network name is also sometimes called the Service Set Identifier (SSID). The network name is usually case sensitive, so make sure you enter it correctly.

4. If the network uses wireless security, choose the appropriate security method in the Wireless Security menu.

5. In the extra fields that appear, as shown in Figure 17-8, enter the network username, password, and other details, as appropriate.

 The exact fields and menus that appear vary, depending on which security method is used. See Chapter 20 for more on working with wireless security.

6. Click OK to log on to the network.

 If you can't log on to the network, double-check that you entered the network name, your username, and any passwords or network keys with the correct case. Network names, passwords, and keys are often case-sensitive.

Figure 17-7: Choose AirPort⇨Other to access a closed network.

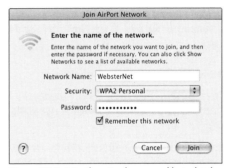

Figure 17-8: Enter the network name and login details here.

Create an Ad Hoc Network between Two Computers

1. Click the AirPort icon on the menu bar and choose Create Network from the menu that appears.

2. In the Computer-to-Computer window that appears, type a name for your ad hoc network, as shown in Figure 17-9.

3. Choose a channel to use for the ad hoc network in the Channel menu.

 Try to choose a channel that's different from that used by other wireless networks in the area. If you aren't sure, just choose Automatic.

4. Click OK to create the network.

5. On the other computer, click the AirPort icon and choose the desired computer-to-computer network, as shown in Figure 17-10.

6. To access the other computer, open a Finder window, click Network in the sidebar, and then open My Network.

7. Double-click the name of a computer that you want to access, click Connect, and log in to the remote computer.

8. When you're done using the computer-to-computer network, click the AirPort icon and choose Disconnect from Current Network.

 To quickly rejoin your primary wireless network, turn off AirPort via the AirPort menu, wait a few seconds, and then turn on AirPort again. AirPort logs on to your default preferred network, if it's available.

Figure 17-9: Name your ad hoc network.

Figure 17-10: Select an ad hoc network to join.

Access an AirPort Base Station from Windows

1. In Windows, choose Start⇨All Programs⇨Accessories⇨ Communications⇨Network Connections.

2. In the Network Connections window, double-click the Wireless Network Connection.

3. In the Wireless Network Connection window, click Set Up a Wireless Network for a Home or Small Office under Network Tasks in the sidebar.

4. In the Wireless Network Setup Wizard that appears, click Next, choose Set Up a New Wireless Network (if you see that option), and click Next again.

5. Enter the network name, as shown in Figure 17-11, and choose the type of security used on your network.

6. Select Manually Assign a Network Key and click Next.

7. Enter the *network key* (the password) and click Next.

8. Choose Set Up a Network Manually in the next screen and then click Next again.

9. Click Finish to complete the setup process and then make sure that your AirPort network appears in the wireless network list, as shown in Figure 17-12.

 To disconnect a Windows PC from your wireless network, double-click the wireless network icon in the Windows system tray (the area in the lower-right corner next to the clock) and then click Disable in the dialog that appears.

Figure 17-11: Enter your network name and choose the security level.

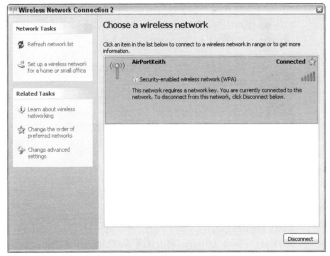

Figure 17-12: Check the wireless network connection here.

Troubleshoot a Wireless Connection

1. Double-check that the AirPort adapter is turned on.

2. Check the signal strength by looking at the AirPort icon on the Menu bar. Four bars indicate a strong signal; fewer bars mean the signal is weak.

3. Check to see if the network is closed. See the section, "Access a Closed Wireless Network," earlier in this chapter for steps.

4. Connect an Ethernet cable between the AirPort access point on your computer and then follow the steps I describe in the section, "Configure an AirPort Base Station," to make sure that the access point is configured properly.

5. Make sure that your computer is configured to work with DHCP, as I describe in Chapter 18.

6. Check that your DSL or cable modem is connected properly to the WAN (Wide Area Network) or modem port on your AirPort access point, as I describe in Chapter 18.

 You might need to connect the modem to your computer to check its status.

7. If you're trying to network wirelessly with a Windows PC, check that your Mac's workgroup name is properly set, as I describe in Chapter 19.

8. Look for devices that may cause Wi-Fi signal interference, such as microwave ovens or 2.4GHz cordless telephones.

9. If Wi-Fi interference can't be eliminated, click the AirPort icon and choose Open Network Preferences. Select AirPort, click Advanced, click AirPort, and then choose Enable Interference Robustness (see Figure 17-13).

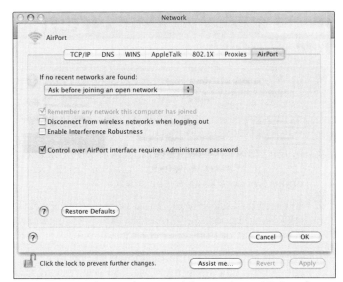

Figure 17-13: Interference Robustness can help you work around Wi-Fi interference.

 Rearrange your hardware so that these items aren't physically close to your AirPort access point or your computer.

Sharing Resources

*T*he number one reason to set up a network is to share stuff among your various computers. This "stuff" usually includes files, Internet connections, and printers. Sharing these resources is pretty easy, as is accessing shared resources on other network computers.

Before you can share anything, your Mac must be properly connected to the network. Chapter 17 shows you how to connect your Mac to a wireless network, and this chapter shows you how to connect to a wired Ethernet network. Ethernet networks aren't quite as convenient as wireless networks, but they offer greater reliability, security, and speed. All modern Macs include adapters for connecting to Ethernet networks.

After you're connected to a network, this chapter shows you how to share printers, files, and Internet connections with the network. Steps also show you how to access shared resources on other networked computers. This chapter shows you how to network mainly with other Macintosh computers, although many of the principles apply to Microsoft Windows computers as well. See Chapter 19 for more on networking with Windows PCs.

Sharing Internet connections, as I describe in this chapter, is usually necessary only if you have dialup Internet access. For example, if you access a dialup Internet service with the modem in your Mac, you can share that connection with the rest of your network if you wish. If you connect to the Internet with a cable modem or digital subscriber line (DSL), the external modem for that service should be connected to the WAN (Wide Area Network) port on your network's router.

Chapter
18

Get ready to . . .

Connect to an Ethernet Network

1. Connect an Ethernet cable between the Ethernet port on your Mac and a local area network (LAN) port on your Ethernet switch, hub, or router.

    If you need to buy new networking hardware, a router is the easiest to configure and provides the greatest flexibility.

2. Restart your Mac and then open System Preferences from the Apple menu.

3. In System Preferences, click the Network icon.

4. Select Built-in Ethernet, as shown in Figure 18-1, and then click Advanced.

5. On the TCP/IP screen, as shown in Figure 18-2, choose Using DHCP in the Configure IPv4 menu.

6. If a numeric IP address isn't listed next to IP Address (as shown in Figure 18-2), click Renew DHCP Lease.

7. Click OK and then Apply to apply your changes.

    To connect two computers together directly without using a hub or router, use a special Ethernet cable — a *crossover* cable. Crossover cables are available at most computer retailers. Keep crossover cables clearly marked because they don't work for connecting a computer to a hub or router. Many newer Macs can connect directly to each other with a regular network cable; check your Mac's documentation to see if it has self-configuring ports.

    If you want to access an Internet connection that's shared by another computer (see the section, "Share an Internet Connection," later in this chapter), follow the steps here to configure your network connection. The Internet sharing server behaves like a Dynamic Host Configuration Protocol (DHCP) server.

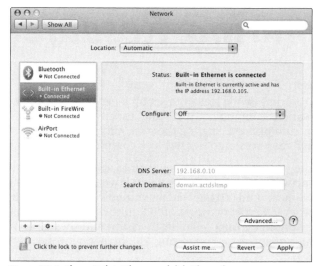

Figure 18-1: Choose Built-in Ethernet and click Advanced.

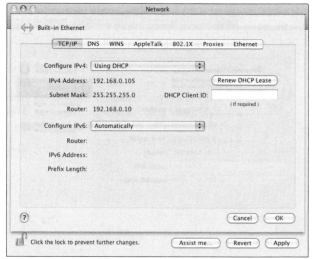

Figure 18-2: Use DHCP when connecting to an Ethernet network.

Set an IP Address Manually

1. Open System Preferences from the Apple menu and then click the Network icon.

2. Select Built-in Ethernet and click Advanced.

3. On the TCP/IP screen, choose Manually in the Configure IPv4 menu, as shown in Figure 18-3.

    If your network uses a router or other DHCP server, but you still need to assign an Internet Protocol (IP) address manually, choose Using DHCP with Manual Address in the Configure IPv4 menu instead.

4. Type an IP address for your computer in the IPv4 Address field, as shown in Figure 18-4.

    On a typical home network, the IP address starts with 192.168.0. The final segment can be any number between 0 and 255. Each computer on the network must have a unique IP address. Check the documentation for your router or server software to see if the IP address should be in a specific range.

5. Enter a Subnet Mask, which in almost all cases is 255.255.255.0.

6. Enter the IP address for the router or server computer on the network. If you don't have a router, enter the IP address for the computer that connects to the Internet.

7. Click Apply Now and then close System Preferences.

    These steps can also apply to AirPort connections and other types of network connections, although usually those connections are configured automatically.

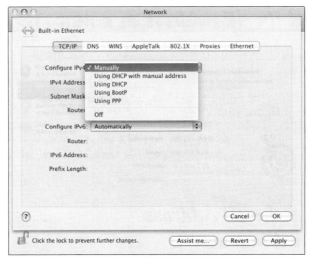

Figure 18-3: You can set your IP address automatically.

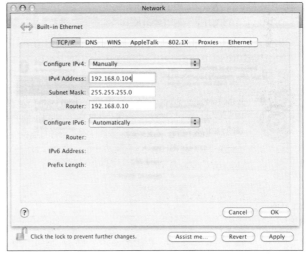

Figure 18-4: Enter the network addresses manually.

Find the IP Address of a Mac

1. Open System Preferences from the Apple menu.

2. Click the Network icon.

3. Note the address listed in the IP Address field, as shown in Figure 18-5.

 The Network screen shows the IP address for whichever network connection is currently active, be it the built-in Ethernet, AirPort, or another connection.

Find the IP Address of a Windows PC

1. On the Windows PC, choose Start⇨My Network Places.

2. In the My Network Places window, click View Network Connections under Network Tasks.

3. Click the network connection to select it and then note the IP address listed under Details in the lower-left corner of the screen, as shown in Figure 18-6.

 If the computer has multiple network connections (such as Ethernet and 802.11 Wi-Fi), make sure you choose the connection that's currently active.

Figure 18-5: This computer's IP address is `192.168.0.102`.

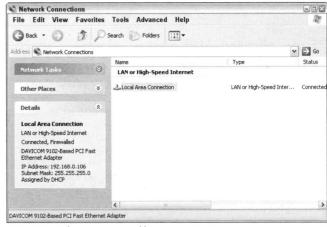

Figure 18-6: This computer's IP address is `192.168.0.106`.

Share an Internet Connection

1. Open System Preferences from the Apple menu and then click the Sharing icon under Internet & Network.

2. In the Sharing window (shown in Figure 18-7), click Internet Sharing to open Internet sharing preferences.

3. In the Share Your Connection From menu, choose the network connection that connects to the Internet. If the computer connects via dialup, choose Internal Modem. If you connect to the Internet with a DSL or cable modem, choose the connection to which the modem is attached. In most cases, this is the Built-in Ethernet connection.

4. Under To Computers Using, place a check mark next to the connection that will be used to share the Internet connection with other computers. This should be a different connection than the one selected in the Share Your Connection From menu.

 Make a note of the warning message that appears when you choose a share-to connection and make sure that sharing your connection doesn't violate the service agreement with your Internet service provider (ISP).

5. If you're sharing the connection using AirPort, click AirPort Options. Select Enable Encryption, choose 128-bit in the WEP Key Length menu, and enter a Wired Equivalency Protocol (WEP) password, as shown in Figure 18-8. Click OK to close AirPort options.

6. Place a check mark next to Internet Sharing to begin sharing your Internet connection.

 The WEP password must be entered on all sharing client computers.

Figure 18-7: Choose the connections to use for Internet connection sharing.

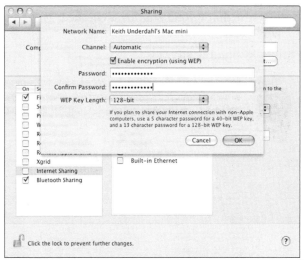

Figure 18-8: Make sure you secure Internet sharing over AirPort.

Share a Printer

1. Open System Preferences from the Apple menu and then click the Print & Fax icon.

2. Click the printer that you want to share to select it.

3. Place a check mark next to Share This Printer, as shown in Figure 18-9.

4. Click Options & Supplies and a descriptive name in the Printer Name field. Make sure that the Location field is descriptive and accurate, and click OK.

 The printer name and location appears on other network computers when the printer is shared, so make sure that the information adequately distinguishes the printer from other devices on the network.

5. Click Show All to return to System Preferences.

6. Click the Sharing icon to open Sharing options.

7. Make sure that Printer Sharing is checked, as shown in Figure 18-10.

8. Close System Preferences.

 Remember, a shared printer can be accessed only when the computer to which it's connected is powered on and connected to the network. The printer must also be turned on and connected to the computer.

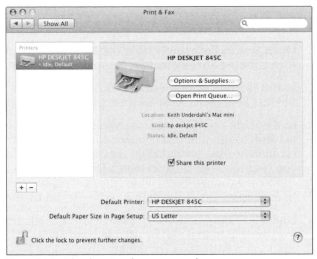

Figure 18-9: Select the printer that you want to share.

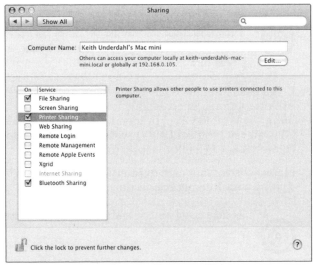

Figure 18-10: Make sure that Printer Sharing is enabled.

Access a Shared Printer

1. Open System Preferences from the Apple menu and then click the Print & Fax icon.

2. Click the Add Printer button. It looks like a plus sign and is located under the list of printers.

3. In the Printer Browser that appears, as shown in Figure 18-11, choose

   - **Default:** Choose this if the printer is connected to a Macintosh running OS X. Select the shared printer and click Add.

   - **Windows:** Choose this if the printer is connected to a Windows PC, as shown in Figure 18-11. Click the workgroup name, the computer name, and enter a valid user name and password for the computer. Then click the name of the printer you want to access. Choose the correct model in the Printer Using menu.

   - **Bluetooth:** If the printer is a wireless Bluetooth printer, choose this option.

   - **AppleTalk:** Choose this if the printer is connected to an older Mac running a Classic operating system.

4. Click Add and then close System Preferences.

5. Open a document that you want to print and choose File⇨Print.

6. In the Printer menu, choose the shared printer to which you want to print, as shown in Figure 18-12, review other printing options, and then click Print.

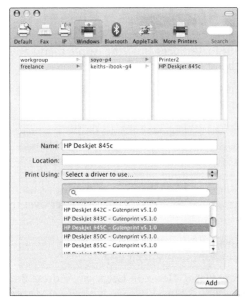

Figure 18-11: Choose the workgroup to which the Windows printer is connected.

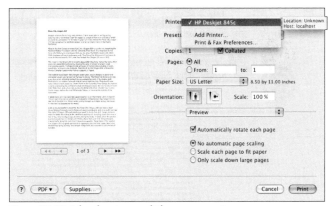

Figure 18-12: Select the printer to which you want to print.

Enable File Sharing

1. Open System Preferences from the Apple menu and then click the Sharing icon.

2. In the Sharing window, place a check mark next to File Sharing, as shown in Figure 18-13.

    Open Sharing preferences and disable File Sharing whenever you access a public Wi-Fi hotspot or other network that isn't secure. This prevents unauthorized users from accessing your files.

3. Click Users next to View By to open the list of users who are authorized to access your computer over the network.

4. Click the Add button under Users (it looks like a plus sign) to add a new authorized user.

5. Select Sharing Users, Network Users, or Address Book to see a list of users. If you don't see the person you want to add, click New Person and enter a username and password in the window that appears.

6. Select the user, as shown in Figure 18-14, and click Select. The user now appears in the list of authorized users in the Sharing window.

    If the network user will access your computer from a Windows PC, see Chapter 19 for more on activating Windows File Sharing.

Figure 18-13: Enable File Sharing to allow others to share your files.

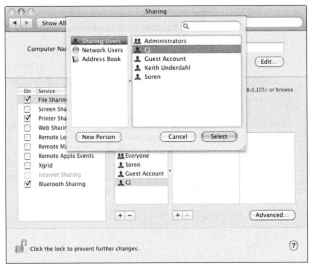

Figure 18-14: Control who can access your computer over the network.

Share Files and Folders

1. Open System Preferences from the Apple menu and then click the Sharing icon.

2. Select File Sharing and then choose Folders next to View By.

3. Under Shared Folders, select a folder for which you want to control sharing. If the folder you want to share isn't in the list, click the Add button (it looks like a plus sign) under Shared Folders and browse to the folder that you want to share.

4. Under Users, select a user, and then choose a level of access for the user, as shown in Figure 18-15.

5. Close System Preferences when you're done sharing folders and managing access.

6. Copy files into your shared folders to share those files.

 Items in your Public folder can be viewed or copied by anyone, so be careful what you put in that folder. Also, don't share other folders on your computer unless you know for sure that the folder's contents are safe for public consumption.

7. Open a Finder window. Under Shared in the sidebar, click the name of a network computer containing shared items.

8. Click Connect As and then enter a valid username and password for the computer.

9. Use the Finder window to browse the computer, as shown in Figure 18-16.

 Choose Guest to log in to the computer as a guest and access public items.

Figure 18-15: Control access rights for shared folders.

Figure 18-16: Access shared folders using the Finder.

Connecting to Windows Networks

*I*t's no secret that most PCs in the world run Windows. You may even have some Windows PCs of your own. If so, there's no reason why your Macs and PCs can't live together. Setting up a network between Windows PCs and Macs takes only minutes; and after configured, you can easily share files, printers, Internet connections, and other resources between the two.

This chapter shows you how to network between Macs and Windows PCs with network hardware that's already in place. The steps here assume that you have

➥ **Mac OS 10.2 or later.** Computers running earlier versions of the Mac OS can connect to Windows networks, but third-party software is necessary. The steps here are based on OS 10.5 or later, but the procedures for OS 10.2, 10.3, and 10.4 are similar. For information on networking between newer and older Macs, see Chapter 22.

➥ **Windows XP or better.** If you have an older version of Windows, you can follow the steps in this chapter to some extent, although some procedures might vary slightly. Windows XP or later provides easier, more secure networking.

➥ **An Ethernet router or wireless network.** For more on setting up Macintosh networking hardware and software, see Chapters 17 and 18. If you need to set up a Windows network, check out my book, *Wi-Fi Home Networking Just the Steps For Dummies* (Wiley Publishing, Inc.).

Get ready to . . .

Set Up Windows File Sharing

1. On your Mac, open System Preferences from the Apple menu and then click Sharing.

2. Type a descriptive name in the Computer Name field, as shown in Figure 19-1. This is the name that other computers see on the network.

3. Select the File Sharing check box, as shown in Figure 19-1.

    File Sharing must be enabled, whether you want to share files with Windows PCs or other Macs.

4. Click Advanced.

5. Place a check mark next to Share Files and Folders using SMB.

6. Place a check mark next to accounts that may access the computer from a Windows PC, as shown in Figure 19-2.

    Only enable accounts that need file access from a Windows PC. Needlessly enabling file sharing for other accounts could compromise the security of your computer.

7. Click Done and then close System Preferences.

    If you no longer need to share files with Windows PCs, open the Sharing preferences window and disable Windows Sharing.

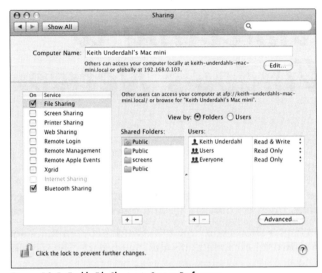

Figure 19-1: Enable File Sharing in System Preferences.

Figure 19-2: Control which accounts can access the computer from Windows.

Change the Workgroup Name on Your Mac

1. Open System Preferences from the Apple menu.

2. Click the Network icon to open Network settings.

3. Select the network connection you use to connect to the Windows network, as shown in Figure 19-3.

4. Click Advanced.

5. Click WINS.

6. Type the name of your Windows workgroup in the Workgroup field, as shown in Figure 19-4.

7. Click OK and then click Apply to apply your changes.

 If you have OS 10.2 through 10.4, setting the Windows Workgroup name is a little more complicated. Launch the Directory Access utility from your Applications:Utilities folder. Unlock the Directory Access Utility using your Administrator password and then place a check mark next to SMB/CIFS. Click Configure next to SMB/CIFS and enter the Windows Workgroup name in the Workgroup field. Click OK and then quit the Directory Access utility.

 To determine a Windows workgroup name, open the Control Panel on a Windows PC and then double-click the System icon. The Computer Name tab of the System Properties dialog box lists the workgroup name. The workgroup name should be the same on each computer on the network.

Figure 19-3: Select the network connection you use to connect to your Windows network.

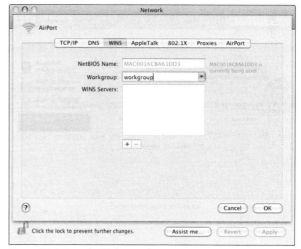

Figure 19-4: Enter the Windows workgroup name.

Connect to a Windows PC from Your Mac

1. Open a Finder window and click Network in the upper-left corner of the window at the top of the Finder sidebar.

     Before you can connect to a Windows PC, both the Windows PC and your Mac should be powered on and connected to the network. File sharing must be enabled on the Windows PC (see *Wi-Fi Home Networking Just the Steps For Dummies* [Wiley Publishing, Inc.] by me for more on enabling Windows file sharing), and you should set the workgroup name on your Mac, as I describe earlier in this chapter.

2. Click the name of the computer to which you want to connect, as shown in Figure 19-5.

3. Click Connect As.

4. Enter an account name and password, as shown in Figure 19-6. The account name and password should be valid on the computer to which you want to connect.

     If you enter an invalid account name or no name at all, you can still connect as a Guest to the Shared Items folder on the Windows PC as well as other shared resources on that computer.

5. Click Connect.

Figure 19-5: Use the Finder to find a Windows PC on your network.

Figure 19-6: Enter an account name and password.

Copy Files from a Windows PC

1. Connect to a Windows PC, as I describe in the previous section.

2. Use the Finder to locate files on the Windows PC, as shown in Figure 19-7.

3. To quickly copy a file from the Windows PC to the Documents folder on your Mac, simply click and drag the file to the Documents icon in the Finder sidebar, as shown in Figure 19-8.

 You can also click and drag items from the Windows PC to your OS X desktop, or you can open a second Finder window and drag files to specific subfolders on your Mac.

4. To copy files from your Mac to the Windows PC, click and drag files and folders to the Windows folder in a Finder window.

 You can't copy files to a Windows folder that shows a small lock icon on the folder image. You can only copy into folders for which you have write access.

When you access a Windows hard drive from a Mac, the Mac OS leaves system file fragments called *resource forks* on the Windows hard drive. These files are unnecessary for the Windows operating system and can be deleted safely after the Mac has disconnected from the Windows PC. See the section on cleaning up resource forks later in this chapter for steps to get rid of resource forks.

Figure 19-7: Windows folders can be accessed through the OS X Finder.

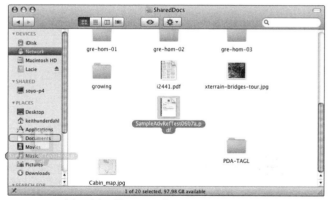

Figure 19-8: Click and drag files to copy them.

Access Your Mac from a Windows PC

1. On your Windows PC, choose Start⇨My Network Places.

    You can also access My Network Places in My Computer or Windows Explorer.

2. Under Network Tasks on the left side of the window, click View Network Computers.

3. Select the Mac to which you want to connect from the list of computers, as shown in Figure 19-9.

    If your Mac doesn't appear in the list, make sure that the Mac's workgroup name has been properly set (as I describe earlier in this computer) and double-check that the Mac is powered-on and connected to the network.

4. Double-click the icon for the Mac to which you want to connect.

5. In the login box that appears, as shown in Figure 19-10, enter a username and password that are valid on the Mac and then click OK.

    In order to log in to a Mac from Windows, you must use a username and password that's valid on that Mac. The account must be authorized to log in remotely, and Windows File Sharing must be enabled on the Mac.

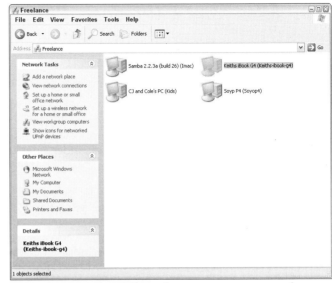

Figure 19-9: Use My Network Places to browse computers on your network.

Figure 19-10: Log in to the Mac with a valid username and password.

Copy Files from a Mac

1. Log in to the Mac from Windows, as I describe in the previous section.

2. Double-click the folder icon for the user account you used to log in to the Mac, as shown in Figure 19-11.

3. Browse to the files that you want to copy.

 Remember, you can only access files owned by the user account that you used to log in to the Mac. Files owned by other user accounts aren't accessible.

4. Select the files you want to copy, as shown in Figure 19-12.

5. Open My Computer or Windows Explorer and then open the folder to which you want to copy the files. Arrange the windows so that both the Mac folder and the target folder are visible.

6. Click and drag files from the Mac to the folder on your Windows PC, as shown in Figure 19-12.

7. Repeat this procedure in reverse to copy files from your Windows PC to your Mac.

 You can also copy or move files in Windows by using the Ctrl+C (Copy), Ctrl+X (Cut), and Ctrl+V (Paste) commands.

Figure 19-11: Double-click the folder icon to access files.

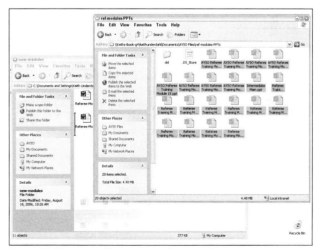

Figure 19-12: Copying files between Windows XP and OS X is easy!

Clean Up Mac Resource Forks on a Windows PC

1. On your Windows PC, use Windows Explorer or My Computer to open a folder that you know has been accessed by a Mac.

2. In the My Computer or Windows Explorer window, choose Tools➪Folder Options.

3. Click the View tab to bring it to the front, as shown in Figure 19-13.

4. Under Hidden Files and Folders, select Show Hidden Files and Folders, as shown in Figure 19-13.

5. Click OK to close the Folder Options window.

6. Identify and select files that have ghost-like icons, as shown in Figure 19-14. These files will have a file name that's similar to another non-ghosted file in the same folder. If you see a file named `.DS_Store`, select it as well.

7. Delete the selected files.

 If you aren't absolutely sure about a file's purpose, don't delete it. Except for the file `.DS_Store`, Mac resource fork files almost always share a file name with another, valid file.

Figure 19-13: Force Windows to show hidden files.

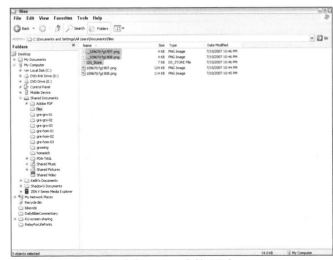

Figure 19-14: Mac resource forks aren't needed by Windows.

Networking Safely

Connecting your computer to a network brings added convenience to your electronic life. Networks let you share files and printers, and connect easily to the Internet. The Internet is the world's largest network, so every time you connect to it you're networking.

But with the added convenience of networking comes some danger as well. With networks, unsavory persons can steal your identity, violate your privacy, access your sensitive files, and infect your computer with viruses. You can avoid these dangers by taking some simple precautions, and this chapter shows you how. This chapter shows you how to

➡ **Create and use network locations.** Network locations allow you to quickly switch to a higher level of security when needed, such as when you connect to a public Wi-Fi hotspot.

➡ **Guard against intrusion with a firewall.** Firewalls block unwanted network and Internet intrusion into your computer.

➡ **Keep unauthorized users off your wireless network.** By changing and hiding your SSID (Service Set Identifier), setting up WEP (good) or WPA (better) encryption, and fine-tuning your wireless transmitter power you can prevent neighbors and passers-by from accessing your network and using your Internet connection.

➡ **Encrypt files.** OS X includes tools to help you encrypt your most sensitive files for added protection.

Chapter

20

Get ready to . . .

Create a New Network Location

1. Open System Preferences from the Apple menu and then click the Network icon.

2. In the Location menu, choose Edit Locations.

3. In the Edit Locations sheet that appears, click the Add Location button (it looks like a plus sign), type a descriptive name for the location, as shown in Figure 20-1, and click Done.

4. Make sure that your new location is selected in the Location menu, click the network connection that you'll use at this location (AirPort, Built-In Ethernet, Built-In FireWire, Bluetooth, or Internal Modem) to select it, and then click Advanced.

5. Adjust network settings as needed for the connection. If you're configuring an AirPort location, click the AirPort button to bring AirPort options to the front.

6. In the If No Recent Networks Are Found menu, choose one of the following:

   * **Ask before joining an open network.** If you choose this option, AirPort asks you before connecting to an unrecognized open network.

   * **Keep looking for recent networks.** This option prevents AirPort from even trying to connect to new, open networks.

7. Place a check mark next to Control Over AirPort Interface Requires Administrator Password, as shown in Figure 20-2.

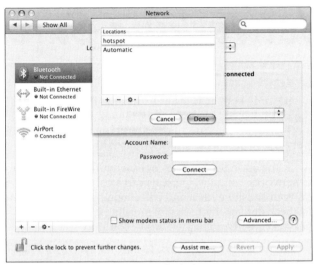

Figure 20-1: Provide a descriptive name for the location.

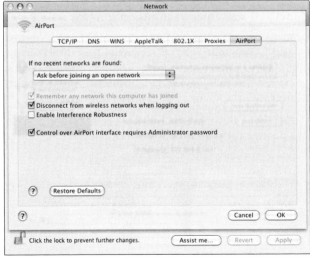

Figure 20-2: Make AirPort more restrictive in less secure environments.

8. Select the Disconnect from Wireless Networks When Logging Out check box and then click OK to close the AirPort options tab.

 If you experience very poor connection quality, look to see if a microwave oven or 2.4GHz cordless phone is near your computer or the wireless access point. These items can interfere with Wi-Fi signals. If you can't separate the items sufficiently, place a check mark next to Enable Interference Robustness. This might slightly reduce Wi-Fi signal interference.

9. If the location has a wireless network that requires a specific login name and password, click 802.1X.

10. Enter the User Name and Password; also enter the network's name in the Wireless Network field, as shown in Figure 20-3. The network name is the network's SSID.

11. Click OK to close the tab.

12. Click Apply to apply your changes and create the new location.

Switch between Locations

1. Open System Preferences from the Apple menu and then click the Network icon.

2. In the Location menu, choose the desired location, as shown in Figure 20-4.

3. Click Apply to begin using the new location settings and then close System Preferences.

 To ensure your security, switch to your more secure location settings before joining a hotspot or other non-secure network.

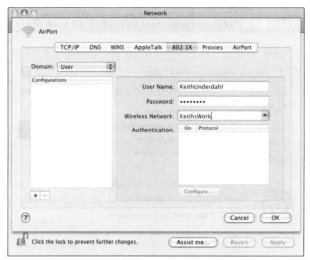

Figure 20-3: Enter security information for a wireless location.

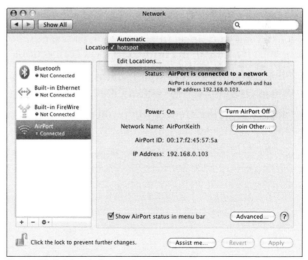

Figure 20-4: Select the location that you want to use.

Protect Your Mac with a Firewall

1. Open System Preferences from the Apple menu and then click the Security icon.

2. Click the Firewall button to bring firewall settings to the front.

3. To block all possible intruders from your computer, choose Block All Incoming Connections, as shown in Figure 20-5.

    If you block all incoming connections, iChat and other Internet-based programs may not work on your system. Choose Block All . . . only as a last resort.

4. To limit incoming connections to only certain programs, choose Limit Incoming Connections to Specific Services and Applications.

5. Click the arrow next to Services to expand the list of services and then use the menu to the right of each service to make a change. In Figure 20-6, for example, FTP connections are being limited to local connections only.

6. Click the arrow next to Applications and adjust connection settings for certain applications as well.

7. Close System Preferences when you're done making changes.

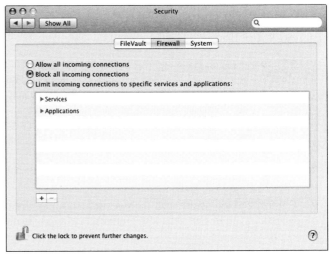

Figure 20-5: Use a firewall to protect your computer from network access.

Figure 20-6: Control which services are allowed to connect to your computer.

Encrypt Files with FileVault

1. Open System Preferences from the Apple menu and then click the Security icon.

> If you're not an administrator on the computer, you must get an administrator's help to enable FileVault because an administrator's password is required.

2. If System Preferences are locked, click the lock icon in the lower-left corner of the screen and enter an administrator password to unlock System Preferences.

3. Click Set a Master Password and then create a master password, as shown in Figure 20-7. Click OK.

4. Click Turn on FileVault.

5. Enter the password for your user account and then click OK.

> FileVault requires a lot of free hard disk space to encrypt files. Double-click the Desktop icon for your hard drive, double-click Users, select your home folder, and press ⌘+I. Make a note of the amount of space used by your home folder. Back in the Finder window, look at the bottom of the window and make sure that the free hard disk space exceeds the size of your home folder by at least 50 percent.

6. Select Use Secure Erase, as shown in Figure 20-8. This ensures secure deletion of files that are sent to the Trash.

7. Click Turn On FileVault. The encryption process might take a while, especially if your home folder is large.

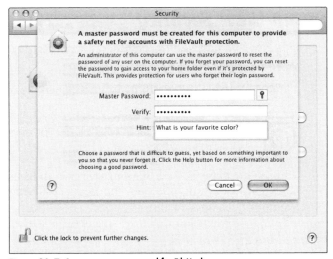
Figure 20-7: Create a master password for FileVault.

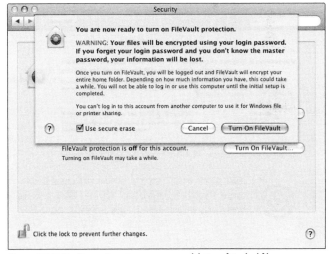
Figure 20-8: Use Secure Erase to ensure secure deletion of Trashed files.

Set up WEP Security

1. Open the Applications folder on your Mac and then open the Utilities subfolder.

2. Double-click the AirPort Utility icon to launch the utility.

 If the AirPort Utility isn't installed in your Applications:Utilities folder, you can install it from the AirPort setup disc that came with your AirPort base station.

3. Choose the network Base Station, as shown in Figure 20-9, click Continue, and then choose Manual Setup from the window that appears.

4. Enter the password for the Base Station and click OK.

5. In the Base Station configuration window that appears, click the AirPort icon to bring AirPort settings to the front.

6. Click Wireless.

7. In the Wireless Security menu, choose WEP 128 Bit, as shown in Figure 20-10.

 WEP 40 Bit may be required for some older wireless computers on your network.

8. Enter a password. A 128-bit WEP password is case sensitive and should be exactly 13 characters long.

 Make a note of the password because you'll need it later. Some devices support only hexadecimal WEP keys. In this case, the password should use only numeric digits 0–9 and letters A–F.

Figure 20-9: Choose the desired Base Station and click Configure.

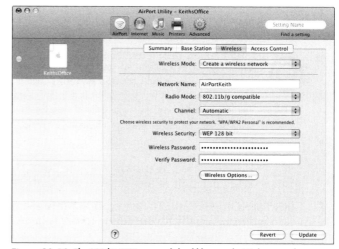

Figure 20-10: The 128 bit WEP password should be exactly 13 characters long.

9. Click OK to close the security tab.

10. Click Update to upload your changes to the Base Station.

11. When the AirPort Base Station has finished restarting (the status light glows solid green), quit the AirPort Admin Utility.

12. On each wireless computer on your network, click the AirPort icon, as shown in Figure 20-11, and choose Other.

 If the name of your wireless network already appears in the AirPort menu, choose that network.

13. Type the Network Name, as shown in Figure 20-12.

14. Choose WEP ASCII in the Wireless Security menu.

15. Enter the 13-character password in the Password field, as shown in Figure 20-12.

 WEP passwords are easily defeated by hackers determined to access your network. Because of this, change your WEP password on a regular basis. Change it at least monthly, or weekly if your network is in close proximity to other potential users.

16. Click Join to join the network.

 WEP — Wireless Encryption Protocol — is less secure than WPA (Wi-Fi Protected Access). Use WEP only if your network includes hardware (such as wireless game console adapters or older computers) that supports WEP but not WPA.

Figure 20-11: Click the AirPort icon and choose Other.

Figure 20-12: Enter the WEP password here.

Configure WPA Encryption

1. Open the Applications folder on your Mac and then open the Utilities subfolder.

    WPA encryption requires Macintosh OS version 10.3 or better. For Windows PCs, handheld devices running Palm OS or Windows Mobile, wireless media players, wireless print servers, and other Wi-Fi devices, support for WPA depends on the manufacturer of the wireless networking adapter. Check the documentation for each respective device to make sure that WPA is supported. If any wireless device on the network doesn't support WPA, use WEP until you can upgrade the offending unit.

2. Double-click the AirPort Utility icon, as shown in Figure 20-13, to launch the utility.

    If the AirPort Utility isn't installed in your Applications:Utilities folder, you can install it from the AirPort setup disc that comes with your AirPort Base Station.

3. Choose the desired network Base Station and click Continue.

4. Choose Manual Setup, enter the password for the Base Station, and click OK.

5. In the Base Station configuration window that appears, click AirPort to bring AirPort settings to the front.

6. Click Wireless.

7. In the Wireless Settings screen that appears, choose WPA/WPA2 Personal in the Wireless Security menu, as shown in Figure 20-14.

8. Type a WPA password. The password should be 8–64 characters long.

 Longer passwords are better because they're less likely to be compromised.

Figure 20-13: Open the AirPort Admin Utility from Applications:Utilities.

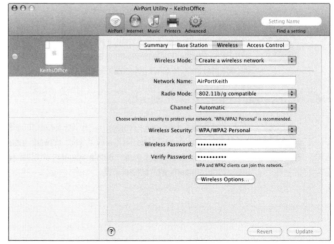

Figure 20-14: Provide a WPA password for your network.

9. Click Update to upload your changes to the Base Station.

10. When the AirPort Base Station has finished restarting (the status light glows solid green), quit the AirPort Utility.

11. On each wireless computer on your network, click the AirPort icon, as shown in Figure 20-15, and choose Other.

 If the name of your wireless network already appears in the AirPort menu, choose that network.

12. Type the Network Name, as shown in Figure 20-16.

13. Choose WPA2 Personal in the Wireless Security menu.

14. Enter the password in the Password field, as shown in Figure 20-16.

15. Click Join to join the network.

 If you're joining a WPA-encrypted network at your workplace or other commercial location, you might need to follow different steps to connect to the site's RADIUS server. Contact your network administrator for details instructions if you have trouble.

Figure 20-15: Click the AirPort icon and choose Other.

Figure 20-16: Enter the WPA password here.

Disable SSID Broadcast

1. Open the Applications folder on your Mac and then open the Utilities subfolder.

2. Double-click the AirPort Utility icon to launch the utility.

3. Choose the desired network Base Station and click Continue. Choose Manual Setup, enter the password for the Base Station, and click OK.

4. In the Base Station configuration window that appears, click AirPort to open AirPort settings, and then click Wireless.

5. Click Wireless Options and then select the Create a Closed Network check box, as shown in Figure 20-17. Click Done and then Update to upload your changes to the Base Station.

 A closed network is one that doesn't broadcast the name or SSID, making it harder for unauthorized persons to join the network.

Reduce Transmitter Power

1. Open the AirPort Utility, as I describe in the previous section.

2. In AirPort Wireless options, click the Wireless Options button.

3. Choose a lower power from the Transmitter Power menu, as shown in Figure 20-18. Click Done and then Update to upload your changes.

 Reduce transmitter power when you're working in close proximity to others — such as in a hotel — and long range isn't important.

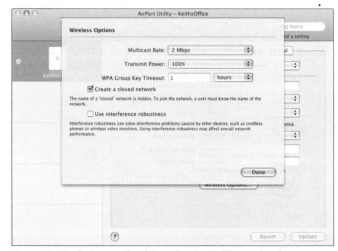

Figure 20-17: The Create a Closed Network option disables SSID broadcast.

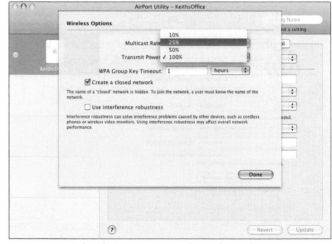

Figure 20-18: Reduce the transmitter power when working in close quarters.

Part 6
Extending Your Mac's Capabilities

The 5th Wave   By Rich Tennant

"Because I can't find my regular cake stand."

Connecting to Bluetooth Devices

*I*f you've been using computers for a while, you're probably familiar with the rat's nest of wires that results when computers and peripherals are connected together. These wires are messy, inconvenient, and prone to loss or breakage. *Bluetooth* is a technology designed to reduce the clutter and inconvenience of wiring by connecting electronic devices wirelessly. Wireless cell phone headsets are the most common Bluetooth devices, but other Bluetooth peripherals include keyboards, mice, handheld computers, GPS antennas, and more. You can even create wireless networks between computers using Bluetooth, although the short range of Bluetooth (usually less than ten meters) makes Bluetooth best suited for peripherals.

Most modern Macs come with Bluetooth technology built-in. This chapter shows you how to

➠ Make your computer discoverable, an important step in connecting to Bluetooth peripherals.

➠ Enable Bluetooth networking so that you can create a temporary Bluetooth network with another computer.

➠ Create connections — called *partnerships* — between your computer and Bluetooth devices.

 If your Mac doesn't have built-in Bluetooth, see Chapter 23 for steps to add an external Bluetooth adapter.

Get ready to . . .

Make Your Computer Discoverable

1. Open System Preferences and then click the Bluetooth icon.

2. Place a check mark next to Bluetooth On if it is not checked already.

3. Select the Discoverable check box, as shown in Figure 21-1.

 If the Show Bluetooth Status in the Menu Bar option is enabled, you can also click the Bluetooth icon in the menu bar to open the Bluetooth menu and enable or disable Bluetooth discovery.

 When working in a public area, disable Bluetooth discovery to hide your computer from unauthorized Bluetooth users.

Enable Bluetooth Networking

1. Open System Preferences and then click the Sharing icon.

2. Place a check mark next to Bluetooth Sharing, as shown in Figure 21-2.

3. In the Folder for Accepted Items menu, choose a folder that may be accessed via Bluetooth.

 If your computer is operated within range of other potential Bluetooth users, avoid sharing private folders using Bluetooth.

Figure 21-1: Enable Bluetooth discovery for your computer.

Figure 21-2: Turn on Bluetooth Sharing.

Send a File via Bluetooth

1. Click the Bluetooth icon on the menu bar and choose Send File in the menu that appears.

2. In the window that appears, browse to the file that you want to send, as shown in Figure 21-3.

3. Click the desired file to select it and then click Send.

4. In the Send File window, click the device to which you want to send the file in the list of devices, as shown in Figure 21-4.

 If the desired device doesn't appear in the list, click Search to find additional devices.

5. Click Send.

6. On the destination computer, click Accept in the Incoming File Transfer window that appears to accept the file.

7. Open the Documents folder on the destination computer to locate the transferred file.

 If the target device isn't a Macintosh computer, the procedure for accepting a file transfer will vary slightly from what is described here, although at some point you should be given a basic Yes or No choice. On computers running Microsoft Windows, Bluetooth-transferred files are saved in the My Documents folder.

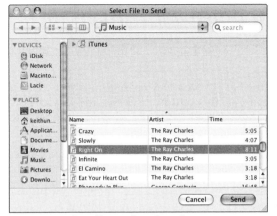

Figure 21-3: Select a file to send via Bluetooth.

Figure 21-4: Select the device to which you want to send the file.

Create a Bluetooth Partnership

1. Open System Preferences and then click the Bluetooth icon.

2. Click the Set Up New Device button, if you see it. If you don't see this button, click the Add Device button in the lower-left corner of the window (it looks like a plus sign).

3. In the Bluetooth Setup Assistant window that appears, click Continue.

4. Choose the type of device with which you want to create a partnership or choose Any Device if no listed type seems to match your device. Click Continue.

5. In the list of devices that appears, as shown in Figure 21-5, click the device to which you want to connect to select it.

6. If the device requires a specific passkey (check the device's documentation), click Passkey Options, choose Use a Specific Passkey in the Passkey Options tab that appears, as shown in Figure 21-6, and then click OK to close the tab.

 If the device is a computer and you want to set up a secure partnership, choose Automatically Generate a Passkey. The Bluetooth Setup Assistant automatically generates a passkey and prompts you to enter that passkey on the device when you finish the setup process.

7. Click Continue and follow the instructions onscreen to complete the setup process. The remaining steps vary slightly, depending on the passkey options you chose.

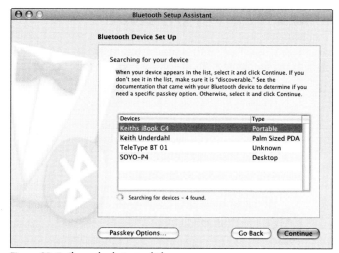

Figure 21-5: Choose the device to which you want to connect.

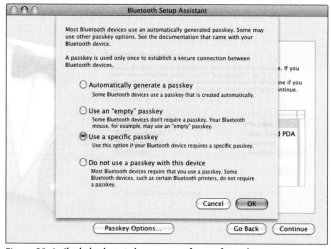

Figure 21-6: Check the device's documentation for specific passkey options.

Networking with Older Macs

Apple is always trying to convince Windows users to switch over to Mac, but a lot of us have already been using Macs for a while. Just because you upgrade to a new Macintosh running OS X Leopard, you don't have to abandon your older Macs to the bone yard. Leopard gets along just fine with computers running older versions of the Macintosh operating system.

This chapter shows you how to network with your older Macs, whether they're running an older version of Macintosh OS X or even a *Classic* version, such as OS 9 or earlier. Tasks show you how to connect to your older Macs from Leopard as well as how to connect to a computer running Leopard from your older Macs. Steps also show you how to set up the network hardware for older Macs that aren't equipped with AirPort cards.

 When this chapter refers to older versions of OS X, the text applies primarily to OS 10.2 or earlier. The networking features in Macintosh OS 10.4 (Tiger) and OS 10.3 (Panther) are functionally almost identical to Leopard, which is also known as OS 10.5.

Chapter 22

Get ready to . . .

Connect an Older OS X Computer to Your Network

1. If the older Mac doesn't have AirPort, select a network router or switch with extra LAN Ethernet ports. Choose one of the following:

   - **Apple AirPort Extreme Base Station:** Choose this if you have only one computer that needs an Ethernet connection.

   - **A third-party multi-port Ethernet router:** Choose a third party router with multiple Ethernet ports, like the one shown in Figure 22-1, if you have more than one computer requiring Ethernet.

2. Connect an Ethernet cable between the Ethernet port on the computer and the LAN port on the router or AirPort Extreme Base Station.

3. Start the older Mac and open System Preferences from the Apple menu.

4. Click the Network icon. In the Network preferences window, choose Built-in Ethernet in the Show menu.

5. Click the TCP/IP tab to bring it to the front and then choose Using DHCP in the Configure menu, as shown in Figure 22-2.

6. Make a note of the number listed next to IP address. You might need this later.

7. Close the Network preferences window and re-open System Preferences.

8. Click the Sharing icon.

9. On the Services tab, select the Personal File Sharing and Remote Login check box.

Figure 22-1: This router has multiple Ethernet ports.

See Chapter 18 for more on network file sharing.

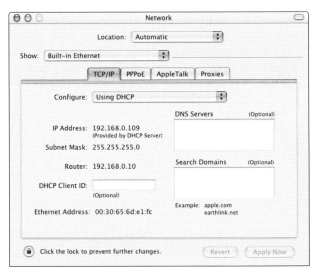

Figure 22-2: Set up your older Mac to work with DHCP.

10. Click the Firewall tab, place a check mark next to Personal File Sharing and Remote Login, and close the Sharing window.

11. With the Finder active, choose Go⇨Connect to Server.

12. Select the network computer to which you want to connect, as shown in Figure 22-3, and then click Connect.

13. Enter a valid username and password for the computer that you're logging in to and click OK.

 When you're done accessing the network computer, drag its Desktop icon to the trash to unmount the network computer.

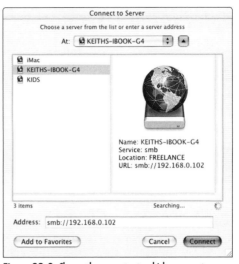

Figure 22-3: Choose the computer to which you want to connect.

Log In to Network Computers from Older OS X Computers

1. In OS 10.3 or later, open the Finder and click the Network icon in the Finder sidebar. Double-click My Network and then double-click the computer that you want to access.

 If you don't see My Network, double-click the Servers icon instead.

Figure 22-4: Log in as a guest or registered user.

2. Log in as a registered user or guest in the window, as shown in Figure 22-4.

3. Choose a volume to mount and click OK.

 If you have trouble logging in, choose Go⇨Connect to Server and enter the IP address of the target computer.

Turn on AppleTalk in OS X

1. In OS X, open System Preferences and then open the Network icon.

2. If necessary, click the network connection that you're currently using and then click Configure.

3. Click AppleTalk to open AppleTalk options.

4. Place a check mark next to Make AppleTalk Active, as shown in Figure 22-5, and choose Automatically in the Configure menu.

Enable File Sharing in Classic

1. On your Macintosh running a classic operating system, open the Apple menu and choose Control Panels⇨File Sharing.

2. Enter an owner name and password, as well as a descriptive name for the computer, as shown in Figure 22-6.

3. Place a check mark next to Enable File Sharing Clients to Connect Over TCP/IP.

4. Click Start to turn on File Sharing.

 When File Sharing has started, select a folder or disk that you want to share on the network and press ⌘+I. Choose Sharing in the Show menu of the Info window that appears and use the options at the bottom of the window to control sharing.

Figure 22-5: Enable AppleTalk in OS X.

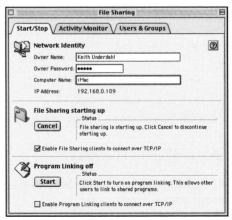

Figure 22-6: Identify your classic computer and start File Sharing.

Connect to a Mac Running a Classic OS

1. In OS X, open the Finder and click the Network icon in the Finder sidebar.

2. Click the My Network icon and then double-click the computer to which you want to connect.

 If you can't connect using the Finder, choose Go⇨Connect to Server and enter the IP address for the computer to which you're trying to connect. You can view the classic computer's IP address via the File Sharing control panel.

3. Enter a login name and password for the computer or choose to login as a guest if you only want to access shared items.

4. Choose a volume that you want to mount, as shown in Figure 22-7.

5. On the computer running a classic operating system, open the Apple menu and choose Network Browser.

6. In the Network Browser, click the arrow next to AppleTalk or Local Network to browse for computers, as shown in Figure 22-8.

7. Double-click a computer and enter a username and password to connect to the computer.

Figure 22-7: Choose which volume you want to mount.

Figure 22-8: Select a computer in the Network browser.

Transfer Your Files to a New Computer

1. Purchase a 6-pin to 6-pin FireWire cable and connect each end to a FireWire port on both the new and old computers.

2. Start the new computer and log in as normal.

3. Turn off the old computer and then hold down the T key while you restart it. The old computer appears as a hard drive on the new computer.

4. On the new computer, open the Applications folder and then open the Utilities subfolder.

5. Double-click the Migration Assistant icon and follow the instructions onscreen to transfer files and other items from the old computer.

 The Migration Assistant works only with computers running Macintosh OS 10.3 (Panther) or later.

Upgrading Your Mac

You've probably heard people scoff at the seemingly high price of new Macintosh computers. But Apple packs almost *every* new Macintosh with a lot of standard features that would be costly options on most Windows PCs. These features include built-in wireless networking, Bluetooth, IEEE-1394 FireWire, and enough RAM (*Random Access Memory*) to ensure good computer performance. If you check the price of a Windows PC that contains all these features, you might find that the Macintosh is actually the better bargain.

Of course, if your Mac is a year or two old, it might lack features like Bluetooth. And no matter how new your Mac is, you might find that you want a little more storage space, screen real estate, or extra RAM to improve the performance and utility of your computer. This chapter shows you how to

➡ **Add an external Bluetooth adapter to a Mac not equipped internally with Bluetooth.** (See Chapter 21 for more on using Bluetooth.)

➡ **Connect to a second monitor.** The second monitor may simply be another monitor to give you more onscreen Desktop space, or it may be a multimedia projector.

➡ **Add external storage space.** If you work with video or need lots of storage space, you can easily attach an external USB or FireWire hard drive to your computer.

➡ **Upgrade your computer's memory.** The easiest way to improve the performance of your computer is to install more RAM.

Chapter
23

Get ready to . . .

Add an External Bluetooth Adapter

1. Purchase a Bluetooth adapter that is Macintosh-compatible.

    Choose an external Bluetooth adapter that connects to a USB port. Internal PCI-card Bluetooth adapters aren't compatible with most Macs.

2. Start the computer and then connect the Bluetooth adapter to any open USB port, as shown in Figure 23-1.

    Mac OS 10.2 or better is required for Bluetooth compatibility. With OS 10.2 or better, Bluetooth software is built-in. See Chapter 21 for more on configuring Bluetooth devices.

Connect to a Second Monitor

1. Connect the appropriate display adapter to your computer, if necessary, and connect all displays to the computer. Make sure each display is powered on.

    New MacBooks, MacBook Pros, and iMacs come with DVI-to-VGA adapters for installing a second monitor. Mac Pros include two DVI display connectors.

2. Open System Preferences and then click the Displays icon.

3. If a separate window for each display doesn't appear, as shown in Figure 23-2, click Detect Displays.

Figure 23-1: Connect the adapter to any spare USB port.

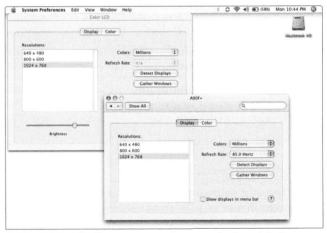

Figure 23-2: You should see a separate Preferences window for each display.

Add External Storage

1. Select an external hard drive that is compatible with your computer.

2. Connect the external drive to your computer's FireWire or USB port, as appropriate.

 USB hard drives are more common, but FireWire (IEEE-1394) hard drives usually offer better performance. If you plan to use the external drive for video editing, choose a FireWire drive.

3. If the drive is formatted using the FAT32 file system (check the drive's documentation), but you don't plan to use the drive with any Windows PCs, open the Applications folder and then open the Utilities folder. Double-click the Disk Utility icon, select the external hard drive in the list of drives, and click Partition. Choose Mac OS Extended in the Format menu, as shown in Figure 23-3, and click Partition in the lower-right corner. Follow the instructions onscreen to complete the partitioning.

 Partitioning erases all data on the drive. Re-partitioning the drive using the Mac OS Extended file system makes the drive perform more efficiently in OS X, but after you do this, you can't connect the drive directly to a Windows PC. Stick with the FAT32 file system if you plan to routinely switch the drive back and forth between your Mac and Windows PC.

4. When partitioning is complete, the drive's icon appears on your desktop, as shown in Figure 23-4. Double-click the icon to browse the drive.

 Before you disconnect an external hard drive from your Mac, drag the drive's icon to the Trash to properly unmount the drive from your computer.

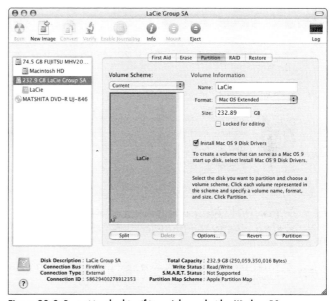

Figure 23-3: Repartition the drive if it won't be used with a Windows PC.

Figure 23-4: The external drive's icon appears on your Desktop.

Install More RAM

1. Shut down your computer. If you have a laptop, remove the battery.

2. Purchase the correct type of RAM for your computer.

    The owner's manual for your Mac should tell you the exact format, capacity, and type of RAM that should be used in your computer. Only use RAM that's positively identified as being compatible with your specific Mac.

3. Locate the RAM slot on your computer:

   • **Pre-Intel laptops:** Remove the keyboard and then remove the RAM access panel, as shown in Figure 23-5.

   • **Intel-based laptops:** Remove the access panel and L-bracket inside the battery compartment.

   • **iMacs and eMacs:** Open the RAM access panel on the bottom or back of the chassis, depending on the exact model you have.

   • **PowerMacs and Mac Pros:** Remove the side cover for the computer case and locate the RAM slots on the motherboard.

    If you have a Mac mini, RAM is less easy to install. You must carefully pry off the top cover with a putty knife and then remove the upper portion of the chassis to access the memory slot. This isn't a simple task and is best left to an Apple repair specialist.

4. Carefully insert the RAM card, as shown in Figure 23-6, making sure that the connector pins and plastic guides line up perfectly.

5. Secure the retention clips and reassemble your computer.

Figure 23-5: The RAM slot on some Apple laptops is under the keyboard.

Figure 23-6: Seat the RAM and secure the retention clips.

Installing and Using Windows Programs

Not so long ago, writing about Microsoft Windows in a book about Macs would've been like school on Saturday: No class. But OS X Leopard introduces a powerful new feature called *Boot Camp*, which allows you to install and run Microsoft Windows on any Macintosh computer that has an Intel processor chip.

"Why would I want to install Windows on a perfectly good Mac?" might be your first question. In most cases, installing Windows will be a matter of *need* rather than *want*. Many software companies still develop products only for Windows, and you may need to run some of those programs for your work or personal needs. To install Windows on your Mac you need

- ➠ **A Macintosh computer running OS 10.5 Leopard and an Intel processor chip.**

- ➠ **10 GB of free hard drive space for the Windows installation.** More space may be needed (I recommend at least 20 GB), depending on the requirements of the Windows programs that you want to install.

- ➠ **A Microsoft Windows installation disc.** It must be a single disc full version (upgrade discs won't work) of Windows XP (with SP2). As of this writing, Windows Media Center Edition and Windows Vista aren't supported by Boot Camp.

This chapter shows you how to install and run Windows on your Mac. Remember, even though you'll be running Windows on stable Macintosh hardware, the Windows installation will still be susceptible to Windows viruses and bugs.

Install Windows

1. Open the Applications folder and then open the Utilities subfolder. Double-click the Boot Camp Assistant icon to begin running Boot Camp.

2. When you're prompted to burn a Macintosh Drivers CD, insert a blank recordable CD in your disc burner and click Continue.

    When the driver disc is done burning, mark it as a Macintosh Driver CD and keep it in a safe place. You'll need it later. If you have several different Intel-based Macintosh computers, create a separate driver disc for each one and mark each disc to identify the computer with which it should be used.

3. When the Create a Second Partition screen appears, as shown in Figure 24-1, click and drag the slider left or right to give the Windows partition more space.

4. Click Partition to start partitioning the hard disk.

5. When you see the screen shown in Figure 24-2, insert your Windows installation disc and click Start Installation.

6. Follow the instructions onscreen to install Windows.

    When you're asked to choose a partition, select the C: drive. The C: drive should be the same size as the Windows partition you create in Step 2. Reformat the drive using FAT32 when prompted to do so. Don't choose the Quick Format option.

7. When Windows setup is complete, insert the Macintosh Drivers CD and follow the instructions onscreen to install the hardware drivers.

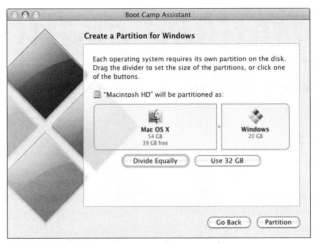

Figure 24-1: Choose a size for your Windows partition here.

Figure 24-2: Boot Camp is ready to install Windows.

Configure AirPort in Windows

1. Boot up the computer in Windows and then choose Start↷Control Panel.

2. If you see a list of categories, click the Network and Internet Connections category. Open the Wireless Network Setup Wizard icon.

3. When the wizard begins, click Next.

4. Choose Set Up a Wireless Network and click Next.

5. Enter the Service Set Identifier (SSID) for your network, as shown in Figure 24-3. If you manually assigned a network key, choose Manually Assign a Network Key. If your network uses WPA encryption, choose the WPA option at the bottom of the wizard.

6. Click Next, enter the network key, and click Next again.

7. In the screen that asks how you want to set up the rest of your network, choose Set Up a Network Manually and click Next. Click Finish to close the wizard.

8. To join a wireless network or manage wireless connections, right-click the wireless connection icon in the Windows *System tray* (the area in the lower-right corner of the screen next to the clock), as shown in Figure 24-4, and choose View Wireless Networks.

9. Use the Wireless Network Connection window, as shown in Figure 24-4, to join or disconnect from wireless networks.

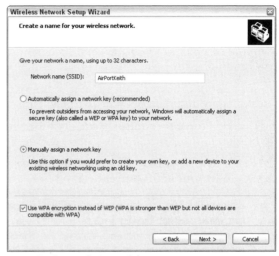

Figure 24-3: Enter the SSID and choose your security options.

Figure 24-4: Use this window to manage wireless networks in Windows.

Adjust Display Settings in Windows

1. Boot up the computer in Windows and then choose Start⇨Control Panel.

2. If you see a list of categories, click the Appearance and Themes category and then open the Display icon.

3. In the Display Properties control panel, click the Settings tab to bring it to the front, as shown in Figure 24-5.

4. Adjust the Screen Resolution slider to change the screen resolution to fit your needs and click Apply.

 When you click Apply, a dialog box appears asking if you want to keep the new settings. Click Yes if you do. If the resolution you choose isn't supported by your Mac's display adapter or monitor and the screen becomes unviewable, simply wait 15 seconds for the display to revert automatically to the previous setting.

5. If the display flickers undesirably, click Advanced.

6. In the dialog box that appears, click the Monitor tab to bring it to the front, as shown in Figure 24-6.

7. Choose a higher setting in the Screen Refresh Rate menu and click Apply.

 Again, click Yes to accept the new setting or wait for the display to revert. A refresh rate of 85 Hertz or better reduces eye strain.

8. Click OK to close the dialog boxes when you're done.

 Use the Themes, Desktop, and Appearance tabs of the Display Properties control panel to change the cosmetic appearance of Windows.

Figure 24-5: Adjust the screen resolution and color quality for better appearance.

Figure 24-6: Choose a higher refresh rate to reduce screen flicker.

Change the Startup Disk in Windows

1. Boot up the computer in Windows and then choose Start➪Control Panel.

2. If you see a list of categories, click the Performance and Maintenance category. Open the Startup Disk icon.

3. Choose which operating system you want to use as the default startup disk, as shown in Figure 24-7. If you choose Macintosh HD, the computer starts in OS X by default.

 If you wish to restart the computer in OS X immediately, make sure that all other applications are closed and click Restart in the Startup Disk window.

Change the Startup Disk in OS X

1. Boot up the computer in OS X and then open System Preferences.

2. Click the Startup Disk icon.

3. Choose which operating system you want to use as the default startup disk, as shown in Figure 24-8. If you choose Mac OS X, the computer starts in OS X by default.

 If you wish to restart the computer in Windows immediately, quit all other applications and click Restart in the Startup Disk window.

Figure 24-7: Control startup with the Startup Disk icon in the Control Panel.

Figure 24-8: Choose the default startup disk for your computer.

Reboot the Computer

1. Save any open documents and close all applications.

2. Restart the computer by following these steps:

    -   **OS X:** Choose Apple⇨Restart.

    -   **Windows:** Choose Start⇨Turn Off Computer and then click Restart.

3. When the screen becomes black during the restart process, hold down the Option key (Alt key on Windows keyboards) and continue holding it until you see a screen like the one shown in Figure 24-9.

4. Use the arrow keys to select the desired operating system and then press Enter.

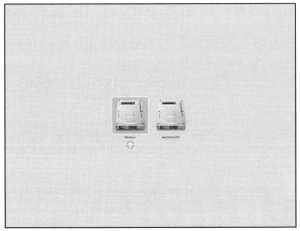

Figure 24-9: Select the desired operating system.

Eject a Disc in Windows

1. If your Mac doesn't have an eject button for the CD/DVD drive, choose Start⇨My Computer.

2. Right-click the icon for the CD/DVD drive and choose Eject from the menu that appears, as shown in Figure 24-10.

 Instead of right-clicking, you can also left-click the CD/DVD drive once to select it and then click Eject This Disk under System Tasks in the upper-left corner of the My Computer window.

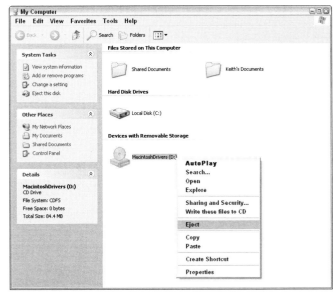

Figure 24-10: Right-click the CD/DVD drive and choose Eject.

Index

• *N* •